REPRESENTATIVE

AMERICAN SPEECHES

1986–1987

edited by OWEN PETERSON
Professor, Department of Speech Communication
Louisiana State University

THE REFERENCE SHELF

Volume 59 Number 4

THE H. W. WILSON COMPANY

New York   1987

THE REFERENCE SHELF

The books in this series contain reprints of articles, excerpts from books, and addresses on current issues and social trends in the United States and other countries. There are six separately bound numbers in each volume, all of which are generally published in the same calendar year. One number is a collection of recent speeches; each of the others is devoted to a single subject and gives background information and discussion from various points of view, concluding with a comprehensive bibliography. Books in the series may be purchased individually or on subscription.

The Library of Congress has cataloged this serial title as follows:

Representative American speeches.   1937/38–
    New York, H. W. Wilson Co.
        v.   21 cm.   (The Reference shelf)
    Annual.
    Indexes:
        Author index: 1937/38–1959/60, with 1959/60;
        1960/61–1969/70, with 1969/70; 1970/71–1979/80,
        with 1979/80.
    Editors: 1937/38–1958/59, A. C. Baird.—1959/60–69/70, L.
    Thonssen.—1970/71–1979/80, W. W. Braden.—1980/81–   O.
    Peterson.
    ISSN 0197-6923=Representative American speeches.
        1. Speeches, addresses, etc., American.   2. Speeches, addresses, etc.
    I. Baird, Albert Craig, 1883–   ed.   II. Thonssen,
    Lester, 1904–   ed.   III. Braden, Waldo Warder, 1911–   ed.
    IV. Peterson, Owen, 1924–   ed.   V. Series.
    PS668.B3   815.5082   38-27962
                                                        MARC-S

    Library of Congress   [8503r85]rev4

Printed in the United States of America

PS
668
.R4
1986-87

CONTENTS

PREFACE

Not unexpectedly, the most important speaking during 1986–1987 concerned the major national and international events of that time. Among the significant topics widely discussed were the American bombing of Libya, allegations of secret arms sales to Iran in return for the release of hostages held by terrorists, covert military aid to Nicaraguan rebels, investment in South Africa, illegal immigration, nuclear arms reduction, and the spread of AIDS (Acquired Immune Deficiency Syndrome).

Political campaign speaking was also important. With the Congressional election of 1986 and the 1988 Presidential campaign in the offing, a great many candidates for public office were busy giving speeches. The speaking in the 1986 Congressional campaigns, unfortunately, did not inspire voters to go to the polls. According to a study by the non-partisan Committee for the Study of American Elections, only 37.2 percent of the voting age population cast ballots, the lowest since 1942. The director of the committee attributed much of the blame to the heavy use of negative political advertising. (Phil Gailey, *New York Times*, November 7, 1986, p. 9) Another disturbing factor in the Congressional races was the way in which Political Action Committees sought influence. Common Cause documented 150 instances in which PACs which had contributed to incumbents' campaigns switched sides after the incumbent lost, showing, according to Common Cause, that the PACs obviously "weren't contributing because of the candidates' philosophy, ideology, or political party. . . . They wanted, first and foremost, to ensure that they had bought influence." (Associated Press, Baton Rouge *State-Times*, March 20, 1987, p. 11E)

At the Presidential level, although campaigning has started earlier and earlier in recent years, aspirants for the country's highest office began speaking and fund raising almost immediately after Ronald Reagan's 1984 victory. Part of the reason for the early start may have been that, for the first time in 28 years, in 1988 neither party would have an incumbent president eligible for reelection. With no incumbent and the unexpected withdrawal of two of the leading Democratic contenders, the race suddenly was wide open for a large number of hopefuls.

The election process itself also was the subject of much discussion. A major concern was the high cost of running for public office. In the 1986 Congressional elections, candidates spent a record near $300 million. In the 1984 Presidential election, the two major contenders spent $134 million. By contrast, the total spent by all candidates in the most recent British general election in 1983 was a little more than $10 million. The high cost of campaigning for office in this country often has meant that candidates must spend more time raising funds than in discussing policies and issues.

The length of campaigns was also an issue. Unlike Britain, where a general election may be completed within 30 days of its having been called, in this country candidates for the Presidency often begin four years before the election.

Since 1960, following the famous Nixon-Kennedy confrontations, televised debates between candidates for public office have become an integral part of presidential, senatorial, and gubernatorial election campaigns. In the past, non-partisan groups such as the League of Women Voters have organized and sponsored these debates. However, over the strong objections of the League of Women Voters, the national chairmen of the Republican and Democratic parties announced they planned to organize the debates involving Presidential candidates in the next election. The southern states' "super-primary," the scheduling of primary elections and caucuses, and television coverage of the campaigns were also issues.

On university campuses, the year was marred by instances of intimidation or outright opposition to the appearance of controversial speakers.

Also characterizing the speaking of 1986–87 was an unusually bitter controversy involving several of the country's most prominent fundamentalist religious groups and their leaders.

Finally 1986–87 was a time of anniversaries: Harvard's 350th birthday, the bicentennial of the Constitution, and the centennial of the Statue of Liberty. All three were observed with appropriate ceremonies and speeches.

In preparing this annual collection of speeches, I rely heavily on the assistance and cooperation of many people. This year I particularly would like to express my appreciation to Barry Cole Poyner, whose enthusiasm and diligence in tracking down information about the speakers and speeches has made this a better volume. I also especially thank Patricia Garcia, who for two years has made my task easier because of her skills as a typist and proof-reader. Virginia Conrad and Lisa Landry have also contributed significantly to this volume. As usual, colleagues at Louisiana State University provided support and helpful advice. I thank Waldo W. Braden, Stephen L. Cooper, Gresdna Doty, Mary Frances HopKins, Andrew King, Harold Mixon, and J. Gaut Ragsdale.

Many others have supplied speech texts and information about the audience and occasion. I appreciate the help of Janet A. Howard, Michael Jackson, Elizabeth Kerrl, Martharose F. Laffey, Karen A. O'Meara, Stig Ramel, Mary Wadsworth, Deborath Weixl, and many of the speakers who provided details about their addresses.

OWEN PETERSON

Baton Rouge, Louisiana
May 26, 1987

ANNIVERSARIES

REMARKS AT THE LIGHTING OF THE STATUE OF LIBERTY[1]
Ronald W. Reagan[2]

A 2½ hour ceremony on Governors Island in New York harbor beginning at 8:30 on the evening of July 3, 1986, kicked off Liberty Weekend, a celebration of the Statue of Liberty Centennial. The event climaxed more than a year of highly publicized and at times controversial fundraising of the $66 million required to refurbish the famous statue, originally given by the French people to celebrate the 100th anniversary of United States independence and Franco-American friendship.

Margot Hornblower described the occasion:

> On a cold, windy platform on Governors Island, with the twinkling lights of tall ships piercing the sunset, President Reagan and French President Francois Mitterand opened the four day, $32 million party of song, dance, fireworks, and patriotic speeches.
> And across the harbor on Ellis Island Chief Justice Warren E. Burger administered the oath of citizenship to 265 immigrants in a televised ceremony that coincided with similar rites for thousands of immigrants in smaller cities across the country. (*Washington Post,* July 4, 1986, p. A1)

Hornblower characterized the program as "in large part a variety show studded with motion picture stars, popular singers, dancers, and other entertainers," noting also that it was "punctuated with awkward pauses to make time for commercials aired by ABC television."

The audience for the ceremony and President Reagan's speech consisted of more than 3,000 corporate guests, from companies such as IBM and Prudential Life, who had paid $5,000 each to attend the ceremony and as many as a billion television viewers in 40 countries.

Nearly 90 minutes into the ceremony, Chrysler Corporation executive Lee Iacocca, who had raised more than $250 million for the renovation effort before being fired from the Centennial Commission by Reagan's Interior Secretary, introduced the President. Following his short speech, Reagan "pressed a button, he and his wife Nancy turned to face the statue, a laser beam shot across the water, and then, from the base up, the statue was brilliantly illuminated in sections." An orchestra and chorus performed "America." The Reagans sang along. The crowd stood and cheered. (Tom Shales, *Washington Post,* July 4, 1986, p. C1) President Mitterand then spoke in French, expressing his pride to be the spokesman

[1]Delivered at 10:00 P.M., July 3, 1986, on Governors Island in New York harbor, New York City.
[2]For biographical note, see Appendix.

of a friendship that has stood the test of time and wishing happy birthday
to the United States and Miss Liberty. At the conclusion of the program,
shortly after 11 P.M., the statue was once again shrouded in darkness. Reagan pressed a second button, her new gilt torch gleamed suddenly bright,
the rest was bathed in light, and the biggest display of fireworks in United
States history shot into the sky.

While the celebration was marred by controversy over the firing of Iacocca, the commercialization of the occasion, and accusations of bad taste,
several political observers commented on Reagan's skill in unifying and
inspiring the American people. Meg Greenfield wrote, "[Reagan] is a genius at mobilizing public sentiments and acting out our national rituals,
legends, and fantasies, the values that we insist motivate us as a people
whether they do or not." (*Newsweek,* July 14, 1986, p. 76)

Time magazine observed:

> Ronald Reagan has a genius for American occasions. . . . Looking
> at his genial, crinkly face prompts a sense of wonder. How does he
> pull it off? . . . Reagan has become a fascinating phenomenon of
> American leadership and psychology. He enjoys an easy and sometimes mysterious communion with the American people. He has become a ceremonial presence. . . . His amiable being—the sheer
> niceness and normality of the man—seems to transcend his policies,
> to immunize him from the poisonous implications of his own opinions. Americans respond to the strength and clarity of his character,
> the predictability of his resolve. . . . Reagan is the first complete
> television President. (July 7, 1986, p. 12ff)

President Reagan's speech: Thank you. And Lee Iacocca, thank you
on behalf of all of America. President and Madame Mitterrand,
my fellow Americans. The iron workers from New York and New
Jersey who came here to begin restoration work were at first puzzled and a bit put off to see foreign workers—craftsmen from
France—arrive. Jean Wiart, the leader of the French workers,
said his countrymen understood. After all, he asked, how would
Frenchmen feel if Americans showed up to help restore the Eiffel
Tower?

But as they came to know each other—these Frenchmen and
Americans—affections grew; and so too did perspectives. The
Americans were reminded that Miss Liberty, like the many millions she's welcomed to these shores, is of foreign birth—the gift
of workers, farmers and shopkeepers and children who donated
hundreds of thousands of francs to send her here. They were the
ordinary people of France—this statue came from their pockets,
and from their hearts.

The French workers, too, made discoveries. Monsieur Wiart,
for example, normally lives in a 150-year-old cottage in a small
French town, but for the last year he's been riding the subway

through Brooklyn. A study in contrasts, he said; contrasts indeed. But he has also told the newspapers that he and his countrymen learned something else at Liberty Island. For the first time, they worked in proximity with Americans of Jewish, black, Italian, Irish, Russian, Polish, and Indian backgrounds. Fascinating, he said, to see different ethnic and national types work and live so well together.

Well, it's how we like to think of America; and it's good to know that Miss Liberty is still giving life to the dream of a new world where old antagonisms could be cast aside and people of every nation could live together as one.

It's especially fitting that this lesson should be relived and relearned here by Americans and Frenchmen. President Mitterrand, the French and American people have forged a special friendship over the course of two centuries. Yes, in the 1700's, France was the midwife of our liberty. In two world wars, America stood with France as she fought for her life—and for civilization. And today, Mr. President, with infinite gentleness your countrymen tend the final resting places—marked now by rows of white crosses and stars—of more than 60,000 Americans who remain on French soil, a reminder since the days of Lafayette of our mutual struggles and sacrifices for freedom. So tonight, as we celebrate the friendship of our two nations, we also pray: may it ever be so. God bless America and vive la France.

And yet, my fellow Americans, it is not only the friendship of two peoples, but the friendship of all peoples that brings us here tonight. We celebrate something more than the restoration of this statue's physical grandeur. Another worker here, Scott Aronsen, a marble restorer, has put it well: "I grew up in Brooklyn and never went to the Statue of Liberty. But when I first walked in there to work, I thought about my grandfathers coming through here." And which of us does not think of other grandfathers and grandmothers, from so many places around the globe, for whom this statue was the first glimpse of America.

"She was silhouetted very clear," one of them wrote about standing on deck as their ship entered New York harbor. "We passed her very slowly. Of course we had to look up. She was beautiful." Another talked of how all the passengers rushed to one side of the boat for a fast look at their new home and at her. "Everybody was crying. The whole boat bent toward her. She was beautiful with the early morning light."

To millions returning home, especially from foreign wars, she was also special. A young World War I captain of artillery described how, on a troopship returning from France, even the most hard-bitten veteran had trouble blinking back the tears. "I've never seen anything that looked so good," that doughboy, Harry Truman, wrote to his fiancee, Bess, in Independence, Missouri, "as the Liberty Lady in New York Harbor."

And that is why tonight we celebrate this mother of exiles who lifts her light beside the golden door. Many of us have seen the picture of another worker here—a tool belt around his waist, balanced on a narrow metal rod of scaffolding, leaning over to place a kiss on the forehead of Miss Liberty. Tony Soraci, the grandson of immigrant Italians, said it was something he was proud to do, "something to tell my grandchildren."

Robert Kearney feels the same way. At work on the statue after a serious illness, he gave $10,000 worth of commemorative pins to those who visited here. Part of the reason, he says, was an earlier construction job over in Hoboken and his friend named Blackie. They could see the harbor from the building where they were working on, and every morning Blackie would look over the water, give a salute and say, "That's my gal."

Well, the truth is, she's everybody's gal. We sometimes forget that even those who came here first to settle the new land were also strangers. I have spoken before of the tiny Arabella—a ship at anchor just off the Massachusetts coast. A little group of Puritans huddled on the deck, and then John Winthrop, who would later become the first Governor of Massachusetts, reminded his fellow Puritans there on that tiny deck that they must keep faith with their God, that the eyes of all the world were upon them, and that they must not foresake the mission that God had sent them on, and they must be a light unto nations of all the world: a shining city upon a hill.

Call it mysticism if you will, I have always believed there was some divine providence that placed this great land here between the two great oceans, to be found by a special kind of people from every corner of the world who had a special love for freedom and a special courage that enabled them to leave their own land, leave their friends and their countrymen and come to this new and strange land—to build a new world of peace and freedom and hope.

Lincoln spoke about hope as he left the hometown he would never see again to take up the duties of the presidency and bring America through a terrible Civil War. At each stop on his long train ride to Washington, the news grew worse: the nation was dividing; his own life was in peril. On he pushed, undaunted. In Philadelphia he spoke in Independence Hall where 85 years earlier the Declaration of Independence had been signed. He noted that much more had been achieved there than just independence from Great Britain. It was, he said, hope to the world, future for all time.

Well, that is the common thread that binds us to those Quakers on the tiny deck of the Arabella; to the beleaguered farmers and landowners signing the declaration in Philadelphia in that hot Philadelphia Hall; to Lincoln on a train, ready to guide his people through the conflagration; to all the millions crowded in the steerage who passed this lady and wept at the sight of her; and those who've worked here in the scaffolding with their hands and with their love, Jean Wiart, Scott Aronsen, Tony Soraci, Robert Kearney and so many others.

We're bound together because, like them, we too dare to hope, hope that our children will always find here the land of liberty in a land that is free. We dare to hope too that we'll understand our work can never be truly done until every man, woman, and child shares in our gifts, in our hope; and stands with us in the light of liberty, the light that, tonight, will shortly cast its glow upon her, as it has upon us for two centuries; keeping faith with a dream of long ago, and guiding millions still to a future of peace and freedom.

And now, we will unveil that gallant lady. Thank you and God bless you all.

THE MANY FACES OF THE BICENTENNIAL[1]
WILLIAM H. REHNQUIST[2]

On February 15, 1987, Chief Justice of the United States Supreme Court William H. Rehnquist addressed the midyear meeting of the American Bar Association in New Orleans. Justice Rehnquist had been invited to deliver the annual "State of the Judiciary" address, a tradition begun by former Chief Justice Burger, but to the surprise of many he chose to speak on the bicentennial of the Constitution.

Although some events had taken place even before the start of the year, 1987 marked the beginning of a four year commemoration of the bicentennial of the United States Constitution. A commission, headed by former Chief Justice Warren E. Burger, was charged with organizing the 200th national birthday. With a budget of more than $22.5 million, the commission plans included special education programs for the nation's schools; an advertising campaign with the theme "The Constitution—The Words We Live By"; and the publication of 3.4 million free, pocket-size copies of the Constitution and bicentennial calendars for distribution to the public. Events marking the bicentennial had been extended by Congress from the signing of the Constitution in Philadelphia on September 17, 1787, to include the separate ratification of the Bill of Rights on December 15, 1791. (Ben A. Franklin, *New York Times*, November 23, 1986, p. 21)

Rehnquist's speech on the bicentennial was his first major address since being named Chief Justice. The subject of attacks by liberals during his confirmation battle, Rehnquist "steered clear of controversy . . . in a low-key address hailing the Constitution's bicentennial." (*Chicago Sun-Times*, February 16, 1987, p. 8) Paul Marcotte observed,

> Rehnquist's low-key speech was a marked departure from those of Warren Burger, who used the State of the Judiciary address in recent years as a forum for strongly worded attacks on lawyer advertising and lawyer competency. (*ABA Journal*, April 1, 1987, p. 1)

Stuart Taylor, Jr., wrote that Rehnquist

> . . . carefully avoided making possibly controversial pronouncements of legal policy . . . , [and] confined himself to a largely historical reminiscence on the bicentennial of the Constitution. He did, however, endorse the need for judges to override the views of elected officials and popular opinion to enforce the Constitution. (*New York Times*, February 16, 1987, p. 1)

Justice Rehnquist delivered his speech at a luncheon meeting in the Grand Ballroom of the Marriott Hotel in New Orleans at 1:30 P.M. on Feb-

---

[1]Delivered at a luncheon at the midyear meeting of the American Bar Association in the Grand Ballroom of the Marriott Hotel in New Orleans at 1:30 P.M. on February 15, 1987.

[2]For biographical note, see Appendix.

ruary 15, 1987. His audience of 2,500 included registrants at the conference and their spouses and families, guests, and press representatives.
The speech was widely covered by the national media.

Chief Justice William H. Rehnquist's speech: This year we commemorate the 200th anniversary of the "signing" of the United States
Constitution. On September 17, 1787, the founding fathers
signed in Philadelphia the charter which, when ratified by the
specified number of states, became the Constitution of the United States of America. Two hundred years after the event, we
know with more certainty than Benjamin Franklin could have
mustered at the time, that his observation about the sun painted
on the back of George Washington's chair being a rising sun, and
not a setting sun, was indeed true. And in this year of the Bicentennial, it particularly behooves those of us who are lawyers to reflect on and speak about the significance of this memorable event.
Lawyers, after all, played a large part in the drafting of the Constitution, and they have played an even larger part in its interpretation.

When we start to think about just what it is we commemorate
this year—what is the significance of the signing of the Constitution—we are in the happy position of having an embarrassment
of riches. First, the signing of the Constitution in Philadelphia
had a historic significance for the United States quite apart from
the contents of the document which the framers approved. Second, the document itself, with all of the shortcomings which we
now see in it, was a remarkable charter which ordained a system
of government which was a vast improvement over the Articles
of Confederation, and in most respects was far more advanced toward democracy and individual liberty than the governments of
the countries from which the colonists had emigrated. Third, the
document as it stands today, a considerably different one from
that which the framers ratified, more perfectly embodies our
present sense of the powers that government ought to exercise,
and the restraints that ought to be imposed upon governmental
power. Fourth and finally, the provisions in the Constitution for
the interpretation of the instrument, and for amendment and
change in the interpretation, were a model of enlightenment at
least equal to any of its substantive provisions.

The "signing" of the Constitution in Philadelphia had a historic significance quite apart from the contents of the document
which the framers approved. It was an important milestone in the

development of the United States as a nation, just as was the Declaration of Independence whose Bicentennial we commemorated in 1976. The Declaration of Independence eloquently stated the reasons for the colonists' revolt against King George III, and committed them to the all-important decision to seek independence rather than reconciliation with the mother country. But the declaration was not itself a continuing source of law, while of course the United States Constitution is. Because of this rather obvious difference, there seems to be a tendency in connection with the present Bicentennial to focus only on the significance of the Constitution as a legal document, and to neglect the historic significance of the fact that on September 17, 1787, representatives from the thirteen states agreed upon a form of government which would bind them together far more closely than they had been.

The Battle of Yorktown, which effectively ended the Revolutionary War, took place in 1781. The Treaty of Paris, which formally ended the war, was signed in 1783. Throughout the period from 1781 to 1789, when the Constitution was finally ratified by the necessary number of states, the only national government of the United States was the Second Continental Congress, operating under the Articles of Confederation. These Articles were seriously defective in a number of respects, the principal one being that the national government could operate only upon the states, and not upon the individual citizens in the states. It was a weak and unsatisfactory form of government, and in those troubled times it was by no means foreordained that the thirteen former colonies would remain united as one nation. Alexander Hamilton, writing in Federalist Paper Number Thirteen, said that "the ideas of men who speculate upon the dismemberment of the empire seem generally turned toward three confederacies—one consisting of the four northern, another of the four middle, and a third of the five southern states."

There was widespread fear that failure to unite would make individual states, or regional confederations of states, a prey to being influenced and manipulated by foreign powers. John Jay noted this fact in Federalist Number Five:

Different commercial concerns must create different interests, and of course different degrees of political attachment to in connection with different foreign nations. Hence it might and probably would happen that the foreign nation with whom the Southern Confederacy might be at war might be the one with whom the Northern Confederacy would be the most desirous of preserving peace and friendship.

James Madison, speaking on the floor of the Constitutional Convention, observed that in the event of the establishment of regional confederacy "Alliances will immediately be formed with different rival and hostile nations of Europe, who will foment disturbances among ourselves, and make us parties to all their own quarrels."

Even without the threat of foreign intervention, problems of finance and trade loomed large because of the absence of an effective national government. States were erecting tariffs and other barriers to trade smacking of protectionism and causing economic stagnation. Those states which had no suitable ports for foreign commerce were subjected to be taxed by their neighbors, through whose ports their commerce was carried on. New Jersey, placed as it was between Philadelphia and New York, was compared to a cask tapped at both ends; North Carolina, placed between Virginia and South Carolina, to a patient bleeding at both arms. In addition, there were serious problems of different currencies among the states and disputes over how the claims to ownership of the so-called Western Territories should be resolved.

These concerns had so troubled many of the thirteen states that a number of them sent out a call for a meeting at Annapolis in 1786 to propose amendments to the Articles of Confederation in an effort to solve some of these problems. The Annapolis Convention was attended by delegates from only five states, and it was unable to accomplish anything substantive by its deliberations. But in what must go down in history as a magnificent combination of boldness and optimism, that body called for the convening of the Constitutional Convention in Philadelphia in 1787.

The reason for convening the convention was to devise "a more perfect form of union." But the success of the endeavor was by no means assured. If it failed, it was not at all certain that the thirteen states would continue imperfectly united under the Articles of Confederation; they might break up into regional confederations. Thus the signing of the Constitution on September 17, 1787, after four months of deliberation, was a tremendous step forward toward nationhood regardless of the provisions contained in the Constitution itself. The very fact that the delegates had been able to agree on a federal government with enough authority to do the job was a milestone in American history. That fact alone gives significance to the Bicentennial of the signing of the Constitution.

When we turn from the significance of the signing in Philadelphia in 1787 as a milestone to nationhood to the provisions
contained in the document itself, we find an instrument with provisions for representative democracy, checks and balances among
the branches of government, and some Constitutional protection
of the individual against the government. At long last it provided
the thirteen states with a federal government adequately empowered to lay taxes, conduct foreign policy, and regulate interstate
commerce. These made it far better than any contemporary system of government with which the colonists were familiar.

But by our present lights the Constitution adopted by the
framers in 1787 had major shortcomings. It implicitly recognized
the existence of slavery, a fact which led the abolitionist William
Lloyd Garrison to describe it as a "covenant with hell." It had no
guarantees of freedom of speech and of the press, or of religious
freedom. It lacked the systematic protection for individual rights
against governmental action which would be remedied in large
part by the Bill of Rights adopted in 1791. So it will not do to regard the Constitution signed in Philadelphia as the "Ark of the
Covenant," immutable and unchallengeable. The Constitution itself wisely contained a provision allowing for its amendment, and
we have had 26 amendments to it adopted by the process specified in Article V.

But just as we should not uncritically extol an instrument
which had these shortcomings, we should not uncritically damn
it either. People in the United States have a great tendency to
judge acts that took place many years ago by standards of present
day morals and values, and this is not generally a very useful endeavor. The Constitution signed by the framers in Philadelphia
in 1787 would not suit us today, because of the drawbacks to
which I have previously referred. But many compromises were
necessary to bring all of the thirteen states on board, and the instrument was a notable step forward in the art of government.
This instrument signed by the founders in Philadelphia is well
worth commemorating on the occasion of the Bicentennial of its
adoption.

Amendments ratified over the preceding 200 years have
largely cured the shortcomings which we perceive in the instrument adopted in Philadelphia. Slavery is outlawed, equal protection is guaranteed, individual rights are protected. But again,
there is no reason to treat our present Constitution with an "Ark

of the Covenant" mentality. Two hundred years from now our present-day Constitution may well seem to our descendants to have many shortcomings which were not apparent to us. These questions depend to a large extent on the temper of the times, and it may well be that although we view the present Constitution as just about right, our great grandchildren will think quite differently about it.

In addition to those 26 amendments ratified and made a part of the Constitution, Congress has proposed seven amendments that have failed to win ratification by the required three-fourths of the states. One of these, I was interested to read recently, provided in part that no law varying the compensation for services of senators and representatives shall take effect until an election of representatives shall have intervened. Another would have authorized Congress and the states to prohibit child labor; the Equal Rights Amendment would have forbidden denial of equality of rights under the law on account of sex. In addition to these seven, there have been many more proposed amendments passed by one house of Congress but not the other. One of these would have forbidden the appropriation of any money or property to any religious body or sect; another would have provided one term of six years for the President; another would have required the ratification of treaties by both houses of Congress. When one reviews the subject matter of these proposals, some seem very dated, and some do not.

Lest we become too sold on the immutability of the Constitution as it stands at any particular time, including right now, it is well to bear in mind that the Eighteenth Amendment granted to Congress the power to enact a national prohibition law, and the Twenty-first Amendment enacted fifteen years later withdrew that power from Congress. The pendulum swung 180 degrees in fifteen years. Proponents of the Equal Rights Amendment have said they will attempt to re-introduce it in the present session of Congress. A responsible organization calling itself the Committee on the Constitutional System has recently urged revision of the First Amendment in order to allow Congress to legislate in areas that the Supreme Court has held were prohibited to it by the First Amendment. Change is the law of life, in government, as well as in other matters.

Thus far I have touched upon three of the four different kinds of significance that the Bicentennial of the signing of the

Constitution has for us: first, it was an important step toward giving us a nation; second, the adoption and ratification of the Constitution gave us a form of government which combined representative democracy and individual liberty in a manner superior to any instrument which has preceded it; third, the Constitution as we know it today, with 26 amendments by which later generations have remedied substantial shortcomings in the original instrument, is a present-day charter which few, if any, of us would trade for any other form of government. But important as all of these three meanings are, the fourth to which I am about to turn is every bit as important as any of the others: the Constitution signed on September 17, 1787, gave us procedural provisions by which the instrument was to be interpreted, amended and changed, which assured both the efficacy and the flexibility of the substantive provisions which it contained. The framers provided for judicial review—that is, they empowered the Courts to invalidate laws which did not conform to the Constitution. This was an original contribution of the thirteen states to the art of government, and was a complete departure from anything that existed in England, from whence most of the colonists had come, or anywhere else in Europe. Lord Coke in the early part of the 17th century had broached such an idea to his mentor, King James I, but that worthy had summarily rebuffed him. The framers, however, wanted to put certain fundamental provisions beyond the reach of change by ordinary legislative enactment. They embodied these provisions in a Constitution, and gave the Judicial Branch of government the final say as to how they should be interpreted.

The members of the Judicial Branch, in turn, were protected against encroachment from the Legislative and Executive Branches by giving them tenure during good behavior and protecting them against reduction in compensation. There was thus established a genuinely independent judiciary. The Supreme Court, sitting at the apex of that judiciary, was made the final arbiter of questions of constitutional law. This was a unique combination of attributes possessed by no other judiciary anywhere in the world.

Because the courts in this country have been so active and so successful in upholding claims of Constitutional rights, there is a natural tendency to think that the words and phrases contained in the written instrument itself are sufficient to assure the protections which they were intended to secure. But a moment's reflection should convince us this is not so. Many nations of the world have very impressive guarantees of free elections, and the like. But these provisions have not had the same meaning in those countries because of the want of an independent judiciary to interpret them. In 1803 in *Marbury* v. *Madison*, the Supreme Court of the United States established the authority of the Judicial Branch to declare laws of Congress unconstitutional. The Supreme Court and other courts have exercised this authority on numerous occasions since that time. The Supreme Court has also unhesitatingly stood up to the Executive Branch when the President sought to act contrary to law: in 1952, it ruled that President Truman acted beyond his Constitutional authority in seizing the steel mills, and in 1974 it held that President Nixon was required to turn over the famous tapes to the courts when they were needed for evidentiary purposes. The tremendous importance of judicial independence in establishment of Constitutional doctrine simply cannot be overstated.

The framers, however, did not stop there. Many of them were conversant with the political theories in vogue at the time, but many were also just as familiar with the vagaries of human nature. They did the best they could for their times, but with great good sense they realized that the instrument which they had drawn and adopted that Summer of 1787 was by no means perfect, and would probably seem even less so to succeeding generations. So they placed in it in Article V a method by which the Constitution could be amended: amendments would have to be proposed by extraordinary majorities of both houses of Congress, and ratified by extraordinary majorities of the states. Change in the fundamental charter was not to be easily had, but as we know, 26 amendments to the Constitution have passed the rather high hurdle required for change.

As I have noted earlier, the framers provided for a thoroughly independent judiciary—the judges were given what amounted to life tenure and protected against diminution of compensation. But the framers, with the uncanny insight which characterized so much of their drafting, did not entirely insulate the judiciary as a whole from popular will. Vacancies in the judiciary were to be filled through nomination by the President, who was responsible to the entire nation, and confirmation by the Senate, whose members were responsible to their respective states. Thus, while individual judges are entirely protected against popular turmoil, the courts on which they sit may have their composition, and accordingly their philosophical bent, changed over time to the process of filling vacancies.

All strong presidents, and some who were not strong, have unhesitatingly used their appointive authority to shape the views of the Supreme Court. Abraham Lincoln did not want to have his actions taken to insure victory in the Civil War challenged before a Supreme bench which was philosophically hostile to the conduct of such a war. Theodore Roosevelt wanted his judicial appointees to be "sound" on the Constitutional issues of his day which were important to him. Franklin Roosevelt was so frustrated by the lack of any vacancies occurring in his first term that he sought to increase the size of the Supreme Court from nine to fifteen in order to get people of his views on the Court.

Thus the framers established an independent judiciary to make certain that the Constitution would not become a dead letter in the hands of judges who were subservient to either the Executive or the Legislative Branches. But they also provided for a method of appointment to the federal judiciary which could in the long run temper judicial interpretations which were believed to be erroneous by a majority of the people. It is this finely tuned mechanism by which Constitutional law is declared, interpreted, and on occasion changed, which is perhaps the greatest gift of the framers of the Constitution in Philadelphia in 1787.

We indeed have an embarrassment of riches to celebrate in this bicentennial year. On September 17, 1787, the framers signed a charter of government which assured us that we would be a continental nation, not a collection of regional confederacies. The charter was drafted by men who realized that time might require changes. They realized that an independent judiciary was essential to give life to the conditional guarantees, and they provided for one. During this year we, as lawyers, should be in the front ranks of those who are celebrating this great event.

"THE SINEWS OF PEACE": REMARKS
COMMEMORATING THE 40TH ANNIVERSARY
OF WINSTON CHURCHILL'S 'IRON CURTAIN'
SPEECH[1]
PAMELA HARRIMAN[2]

While special occasions commemorating anniversaries of the birth or death of a famous person, the date of an important historical event, or an important discovery or invention are not unusual, meetings honoring the delivery of a speech are rare. But on May 19, 1986, a group of Americans met in New York City to commemorate an address given 40 years earlier in a small Missouri town by a former British prime minister. The speech was Winston Churchill's "The Sinews of Peace"—better known as the "Iron Curtain" speech—given at Westminster College in Fulton, Missouri, on March 5, 1946. The speaker was Pamela Harriman.

Mrs. Harriman was eminently qualified to discuss the meaning and significance of the speech. Educated in England and France, the former Pamela Digby had married Randolph Churchill and, as daughter-in-law of Prime Minister Winston Churchill, had served as his hostess at 10 Downing Street during World War II. Years later, following the death of her husband, she married W. Averell Harriman, the former American ambassador to Great Britain and the Soviet Union, ambassador-at-large, governor of New York, and advisor to Franklin D. Roosevelt at Teheran and Yalta. As a naturalized American, Mrs. Harriman has been very active politically, serving on several Democratic party committees. In 1980 she cofounded, with her late husband, "Democrats for the '80s," an organization devoted to electing Democrats and helping the party prepare for the future.

In her address, Mrs. Harriman sought to correct some misconceptions about Churchill's speech at Westminster College in 1946. She explained:

> When he spoke 40 years ago of the "Iron Curtain" that had descended from "Stettin in the Baltic to Trieste in the Adriatic," Winston Churchill was acknowledging and announcing a truth that so many in the West were so unwilling to admit—the onset of the Cold War. So powerful was the phrase and so pronounced was the turning point marked by this speech that leaders have been returning to it ever since to validate their own policies. (Pamela C. Harriman, "What Churchill Really Said," *Washington Post*, May 25, 1986)

Unfortunately, according to Mrs. Harriman, Churchill's speech has been misunderstood and misinterpreted. "What did he really say at Fulton, Missouri—what did he mean—and how does it apply today?" she asked. She cited three points Churchill made at Fulton which apply with equal

---

[1]Delivered at a luncheon meeting in the Cotillion Room of the Hotel Pierre in New York City at 1:30 P.M. on May 19, 1986.
[2]For biographical note, see Appendix.

force today, but which she argued do not seem to be clearly heard and heeded in the councils of power. These were, "First, the address was a plea for peace, not conflict. . . . Second, . . . that there was a basis on which to deal with the Soviets. . . . Third, Winston Churchill was convinced that the West should actively pursue what he called 'a good understanding with the Russians.'" However, most hardliners, according to Mrs. Harriman, misconstrue or conveniently ignore these counsels.

Mrs. Harriman delivered her remarks at a luncheon meeting in the Cotillion Room of the Hotel Pierre in New York City at 1:30 P.M. on May 19, 1986 to approximately 300 persons. In addition to commemorating the 40th anniversary of Churchill's speech, the luncheon also honored The Winston Churchill Memorial and Library in the United States at Westminster College in Fulton, Missouri. Among those present were the Consul General of Britain James Mellon, members of the New York Chapter of Friends of the Winston Churchill Memorial, and many distinguished New Yorkers.

The speech was covered by the *Washington Post*, the *International Herald Tribune*, and Flora Lewis in the *New York Times*, and was inserted in the *Congressional Record*.

Pamela Harriman's speech: Today we honor the anniversary of an event, which, like so many in Winston Churchill's life, was accounted as an historic moment, and yet the man himself was out of power. He was unique among the leaders of twentieth century democracy in that his influence did not disappear with his office. Perhaps his only rival in this respect was General DeGaulle—who pales by comparison with Churchill's capacity to stand astride the world stage, even while relegated to the backstage of opposition in his own country.

This role had not come easily or early to Churchill. In his long political exile of the 1930s, he was a lonely voice, "crying in the wilderness," and few turned to hear him or to see the approaching storm. Yet he never tired, for he always knew that history, too, had its claims. Perhaps he understood that because he wrote history as much as he made it. He was an author as well as an orator. He was not only a prime minister, he was also a prophet of things to come.

It was this unique ability that he took with him to Fulton, Missouri, forty years ago last March. Winston Churchill made his mistakes; but he was more often right than wrong on more matters of consequence than any other statesman of this century.

He was not only an early, isolated critic of appeasement. He was also one of the first, perhaps the first non-scientist, to comprehend and describe the dawning wonders and terrors of modern invention. In a 1932 essay—more than a decade before the

Manhattan project—he speculated, "that new sources of energy, vastly more important than any we yet know, will surely be discovered. . . . Nuclear energy is incomparably greater than the molecular energy we use today. . . . There is no question that this gigantic source of energy exists. What is lacking is the match to set the bonfire alight, or it may be the detonator to cause the dynamite to explode."

He wrote of "wireless telephones and televisions" and of genetic engineering. He looked to a time, "fifty years hence," when "explosive machinery will be available upon a scale which can annihilate whole nations." In 1925, he wrote of "guided missiles" and of "electrical rays which could claw down aeroplanes from the sky."

Churchill was different from most political leaders in that he thought beyond the next election to the next generation. It was this sense of perspective which enabled him to persevere despite recurring disappointments in his public life. His moment of triumph did not come until he was sixty-five, the normal retirement age, and long after he had been written off. In its greatest trial, Britain found its greatest modern leader. Yet five years later, with the war won, he was defeated for reelection. He had the world's honor and respect, but not his country's vote.

So it was that a year after that, President Truman invited Winston Churchill—as prophet and not prime minister—to speak in Truman's home state, at Westminster College, "a name," as Churchill said, "somewhat familiar to me." It was five thousand miles from the Parliament at Westminster to this midwestern college podium. And the speaker of the day brought with him one of the most famous speeches of all time, a speech which is so often cited as a text for our time.

When he spoke of the "Iron Curtain" that had descended from "Stettin in the Baltic to Trieste in the Adriatic," Winston Churchill was acknowledging and announcing a truth which so many in the West were so unwilling to admit: the onset of the Cold War. So powerful was the phrase, it cut like a thunderbolt through the public dialogue; so pronounced was the turning point marked by this speech; so wise does it seem, at least in retrospect, that leaders since then return to it and quote it repeatedly to validate their own policies.

Half of the lectures delivered since 1946 in the Westminster series, in which Churchill spoke, have been primarily or partly commentaries on his speech. Presidents, vice-presidents, cabinet officials, senators, ambassadors, and one other British prime minister have followed in his footsteps.

All this, I suspect, would evoke from Churchill a reaction something like Lincoln's description of the man tarred and feathered and ridden out of town on a rail: "If it wasn't for the honor of the thing, I'd rather walk." Winston Churchill sought to be memorable, but I am certain that he would rather be remembered for what he actually said and believed, and not have his remarks misused as an all-purpose proof text for the prevailing policies of the hour. He spoke so often and so well over so many years that by taking selected words out of their context, or whole speeches out of the context of their times, virtually anyone who is clever enough can quote Churchill to suit his own purposes.

So what did he really say at Fulton, Missouri, what did he mean, and how does it apply today?

First, as one of the architects of the Grand Alliance, he, in effect, recognized the tragic reality of its dissolution. No one else of similar authority had said what he did so plainly or so publicly before. And this, too, he had foreseen. At the Cairo Conference in 1943, he told Harold MacMillan of his fears about the rise of Soviet power and the failure of the West to observe and respond to the danger.

Second, he traced the roots of the dawning conflict to Soviet territorial ambitions. As he put it, "What they desire is the fruits of war and the indefinite expansion of their power and doctrines."

Power *and* doctrine: Winston Churchill had read history and he knew that ideology was not simply or solely the reason for Soviet aggression and subversion; it was, in sinister combination, the rationalization of conquests otherwise coveted. The Soviet commissars were fulfilling, on a grander scale, the expansionist ambitions of the Russian czars. This continuing, expansionist impulse was felt in Eastern Europe in the 1940s; it is felt in Afghanistan today.

Third, he urged the West to be firm—in the form of both closer British-American association and a new European unity—from which, he said, "no nation should be outcast." Already, again prophetically, he was anticipating the then almost unimaginable rapprochement between France and Germany. Most of all, Churchill gently warned, firmness required American involvement; we cannot afford, he said in politer words than these, a repetition of the catastrophic American retreat from international responsibility after World War I.

He saw the emerging parallel in 1946; in less than a year, the United States Army had shrunk by nearly 90 percent. The boys were coming home, but Churchill was reminding us that now all Europe and the world were our neighborhood.

He was looking toward a system of collective security; he was anticipating NATO by three years, each year marked by recurrent and escalating crisis with the Soviet Union. So he asked the Western powers "to stand together," and he concluded: "There is nothing [the Russians] admire so much as strength, and there is nothing for which they have less respect than weakness, especially military weakness."

It is at this point, for the most part, that the reading, citation, and interpretation of the Fulton speech all stop. Probably that is because it was Churchill's sounding of the alarm about Soviet misdeeds which drew the most attention and the most controversy at the time. Indeed that aspect of the speech aroused nearly violent protest among many Americans, who once again were hoping that they had finished the war to end all wars. In New York a few days after Fulton, the police had to be called out to protect the former British prime minister from hostile demonstrators parading outside the Waldorf-Astoria, where he was staying.

To the extent the "Iron Curtain" speech is seen and cited as a powerful and historic warning against an emerging and ruthless adversary, we can say of this interpretation: so far, so true. We can largely say this, even when, as frequently happens, the interpretation ignores the subtleties of Churchill's argument. But if we stop here, if that is all we see in the speech, then all we are getting is a half-truth.

There are three other points Winston Churchill made at Fulton which apply with equal force today, but which do not seem to be as clearly heard and heeded in the councils of power.

First, the address was a plea for peace, not conflict. It began with the reminder that "our supreme task and duty is to guard the homes of the common people from the horrors and miseries of another war." Churchill viewed that prospect with undisguised apprehension. He spoke of future world conflict, and I quote, "as incomparably more rigorous than what the world had just been through. The Dark Ages may return, the Stone Age may now return on the gleaming wings of science, and what might shower immeasurable material blessings upon mankind may even bring about its total destruction."

Forty years ago, when the West held a temporary nuclear monopoly, Churchill was not talking of "winnable" nuclear wars; he was worried about nuclear wars in which the only winner would be death. And to him, even then, the issue was urgent: "Beware I say; time may be short. Do not let us take the course of allowing events to drift along until it is too late."

Second, the former and future prime minister insisted that there was a basis on which to deal with the Soviets. He had stated it before, shortly after the outbreak of the war in 1939. In another famous phrase which is also usually only half-quoted, he said, "Russia . . . is a riddle, wrapped in a mystery, inside an enigma; but perhaps there is a key. The key is Russian national interest."

The part about national interest is invariably the part of the speech that is left out. But in 1946, at Fulton, Churchill identified precisely what that interest was: The Soviets might want expansion, but they did not want war. The inevitable truth of that principle, in the atomic age, still eludes foolish and dangerous people on both sides of the Iron Curtain, who assume that on the other side, a first strike is being planned, a nuclear exchange is being actively considered—and therefore, arms control is an impossible dream or an undesirable snare. To them, Churchill replied, forty years in advance: "What we have to consider . . . is the permanent prevention of war." This, he believed, was in the Russian interest as surely as our own.

Third, Winston Churchill was convinced that the West should actively pursue what he called "a good understanding with the Russians. . . . There is the solution which I would offer to you . . . ."

He was to expand on this theme again and again. At the Conservative party conference in North Wales in 1949, during the most frigid days of the Cold War, he called on the West to take the initiative in opening talks with the Soviets. This time, it was the hawks who assailed him. They and their ideological descendants prefer to edit Fulton, to forget the party conference, and to neglect the sweeping proposal of Churchill's second prime ministership in 1953.

After Stalin's death in March of that year, the new Soviet regime appeared to Churchill to be signalling, in various ways—for example, in the Austrian treaty negotiations—a new readiness to reduce tensions. He believed there was at least a glimmer of light, a possibility of progress. He told President Eisenhower in a letter: "A new hope has been created in the unhappy, bewildered world." And he suggested that the West make a new approach to Moscow. He wrote in a top secret message: "If we fail to . . . seize this moment's precious chances, the judgment of future ages would be harsh and just."

The moment, unfortunately, remained unseized. John Foster Dulles and some in the British Foreign Office accused Winston Churchill of starting down the road to appeasement. As the recently published diary of his private secretary, Sir John Colville, recounts, it was one of the bitter moments of Churchill's life when Eisenhower rejected the policy of negotiation.

The issue is not whether the policy surely would have worked; many of his friends conceded that at that time it might very well have failed. But Winston Churchill was steadfast in believing that it should be tried. As he said in 1955, in one of his last, great speeches to Parliament, "I have hoped for a long time for a top-level conference where these matters can be put plainly and bluntly," and he was talking then specifically about the issue of nuclear weapons.

This is the complete Churchill, not the hardliners' conveniently quotable half. He was, I believe, right about the Soviet danger and the nuclear danger. He was right to warn against appeasement, and equally right to warn against a rigid, all or nothing approach to the Russians. Today his insights, in their full form, still have the freshness of morning, a crispness which has not wilted with the years. But we cannot have his counsel about the Soviets without his counsel about ourselves: the two parts are of a single piece, shaped by a single, subtle mind, the product of a complex and realistic world view.

Across four decades, Winston Churchill's voice and his advice still speak to us and they come down to this: yes, you can deal with the Russians, but only if you have both strength and suppleness, a willingness to stand your essential ground, and yet to see a great common interest which transcends inevitable rivalries, regional conflicts, and petty quarrels.

Now the question is, how have we applied this prescription in the long passage of time since the Fulton speech? Sometimes not at all, sometimes with great uncertainty, and always with great inconsistency.

In his brief years in office, President Kennedy, who took a special pleasure in conferring the first honorary American citizenship on Winston Churchill, became the post-war American leader who seemed to understand best the Churchill formula of toughness and negotiation. One October, he prevailed in the Cuban missile crisis, a victory which he then used as an opportunity to seek a test ban treaty. By the next July, he had sent Averell Harriman to Moscow to conclude the agreement.

It was in many ways a fitting choice of a negotiator, not least in terms of our topic today: Just after the Fulton speech, Churchill and Harriman met in Washington for a long private talk. Harriman shared Churchill's conclusion, as he reported it in his notes, that he "was very gloomy about coming to any accommodation with Russia unless and until it became clear to the Russians that they would be met by force if they continued their expansion. . . . " Seventeen years later, after the Soviet installation of missiles in Cuba had been met and repulsed, it was Averell Harriman who initialled, for the United States, the first great formal accommodation of the post-war era.

Most of the time, however, we appear to have followed only half the lesson of this history—to stand fast—and not the other half—that the stand should not be a stopping place, but a departure point toward making the world safer for human survival. Each tough stand, once taken, should be another step in the thousand mile journey toward peace.

A number of observers had believed—or hoped—that in his second term, Ronald Reagan could and would move in this direction. He certainly does have the same kind of freedom of action Richard Nixon did when he reopened the door to China: no one could accuse *him* of being soft. Mr. Reagan surely would not encounter the attacks from the right visited on Gerald Ford when he tried to negotiate SALT-II as the 1976 Republican primaries neared. He certainly would have a far more receptive Senate than Jimmy Carter found when he submitted an arms agreement in 1979.

Just as a certain measure of strength is a precondition for negotiating a treaty with the Soviets, so perhaps a certain measure of perceived toughness is a precondition for securing its approval here at home. Ronald Reagan undoubtedly meets that test. Over and over again, from the beginning of his administration, he has attacked the Soviets as the "focus of evil in the world" and he has constantly urged larger and larger defense budgets to meet the Soviet threat.

Yet the President and his Secretary of Defense, so intent on demonstrating their resolve, so fond of quoting Churchill, seem increasingly reluctant to take the full measure of Churchill's advice. The administration talks of arms control; under public pressure, the President speaks of the unwinnability of nuclear war. But our negotiations in Geneva so far resist any compromise on the Star Wars concept, even in return for the most comprehensive strategic arms agreement. When the Russians concede ground on the question of intermediate range missiles in Europe, and agree to a treaty in this area regardless of what happens on Star Wars, the administration responds by restating its own previous position.

Winston Churchill had a purpose in his strategy of deploying strength in dealing with the Soviets. He was, as Sir John Colville says, a leader who adopted a "flexibility" which "may have a certain relevance in the 1980s." His aim, as he himself expressed it in the Fulton speech, never wavered: he said, "What is needed is a settlement, and the longer this is delayed, the more difficult it will be and the greater our dangers will become." To Churchill, military strength, divisions, missiles were not an end in themselves; he armed in order to parley.

On the fortieth anniversary of the Fulton speech, in the sixth year of the Reagan Administration, it is fitting and fair to ask of them: What is the aim of their policy? Do they expect, by military intimidation or economic exhaustion, to bring the Soviet system down, something that Churchill, one of the original anti-Bolsheviks, considered foolhardy in the atomic age? If so, do they expect the Soviets to go gently into the twilight of their diminishing power, or abjectly accept an internal collapse?

These are not realistic hopes, but dangerous fantasies, and we should pray that no one in office really has such irrational views. Perhaps the administration's stubbornness is a bargaining strategy. But the strategy can be justified only if, at the end of the negotiating process, there is a negotiated agreement.

I would be more encouraged if the President would read the entire Fulton speech and Winston Churchill's other post-war writings. He would discover that the spirit of Winston Churchill was one of both resolution and conciliation; of magnanimity based on strength, and that is the spirit the world urgently needs today.

In short, we should recall that Churchill entitled his Fulton speech "The Sinews of Peace," not war. And I would like to close with some words which he was composing at nearly the same time he was drafting the speech. He wrote:

Those who are prone by temperament and character to seek sharp and clear-cut solutions of difficult and obscure problems, who are ready to fight whenever some challenge comes from a foreign Power, have not always been right. On the other hand, those whose inclination is to bow their heads, to seek patiently and faithfully for peaceful compromise, are not always wrong. On the contrary, in the majority of instances they may be right, not only morally but from a practical standpoint. How many wars have been averted by patience and persisting good will! . . . How many wars have been precipitated by firebrands! How many misunderstandings which led to war could have been removed by temporizing! How often have countries fought cruel wars and then after a few years of peace found themselves not only friends but allies!

These words are from the first volume of Winston Churchill's World War II memoirs, in preparation even as he traveled to Missouri. He called the volume *The Gathering Storm*. We would be well advised today to heed his warning, to hear the real Churchill voice and views.

For now we must deal with the potentially even more cataclysmic storm gathering in our own time.

HAPPY 350TH BIRTHDAY, FAIR HARVARD![1]
Derek Bok[2]

Thousands of alumni and friends, along with dignitaries from around the world, gathered in Cambridge, Massachusetts, for four days in September 1986 to celebrate the 350th anniversary of the founding of Harvard College and the birth of American higher education.

The celebration "was marked by speeches, black-tie dinners, shouts and squeals of recognition, fireworks, concerts, exhibits, dance recitals, and all the pomp and ceremony a university of Harvard's stature could muster." (Zoe Ingalls, *Chronicle of Higher Education*, September 10, 1986, p. 40) Britain's Prince of Wales was the featured speaker at a "Foundation Day" meeting—the first of three convocations—that drew a capacity audience of 18,000 people. Speakers at the other two convocations were

[1]Delivered in the Tercentenary Theatre in Harvard Yard, Cambridge, Massachusetts, at 2:00 P.M. on September 6, 1986.
[2]For biographical note, see Appendix.

Secretary of State George P. Shultz and Harvard President Derek Bok.

In addition, Harvard faculty members and distinguished visiting scholars gave 105 symposia on topics ranging from biomolecular processes to the world market. Participants included governors, senators, congressional representatives, cabinet members, and Supreme Court justices. Other major events included a closing night extravaganza of entertainment and fireworks with more than 700 performers, including the Boston Pops Orchestra. Walter Cronkite served as master of ceremonies.

The anniversary observance was the subject of widespread media coverage because of the eminence of the university. *U.S. News and World Report* called Harvard "America's oldest and most esteemed institution of higher learning." (August 25, 1986, p. 46) *Time* said that it "ranks as one of the world's most distinguished centers of learning." (September 8, 1986, p. 64) Ernest Boyer, president of the Carnegie Foundation for the Advancement of Teaching, observed, "Harvard has shaped the world of higher education. . . . It's the cathedral that provides inspiration for all others." (*U.S. News and World Report,* April 25, 1986, p. 46) Further attesting to the school's reputation, the Harvard faculty has produced 29 Nobel laureates and 27 Pulitzer Prize winners. Six United States presidents were alumni.

On the final day of the celebration, September 6, called "Alumni Day," Harvard President Derek Bok addressed an audience estimated at between 17,000 and 18,000 in Harvard Yard at the last of the three convocations. He delivered his speech at 2:00 P.M. in the Tercentenary Theatre.

Bok, Harvard's 25th president, has one thing in common with its first chief, unlike all the 23 men between them: neither was a Harvard undergraduate. But Bok, from Stanford, does have a Harvard law degree. Bok became president of Harvard in 1971 at the age of 41. In a profile, *Time* described him as follows:

> Though affable and articulate, Bok was and is a very private man. . . . Yet in the course of his tenure, Bok has successfully steered Harvard through some enormous changes. . . . No Harvard president could remain totally immune to criticism, . . . but on balance he wins high marks. (September 8, 1986, p. 63)

In his address, Bok warned of the dangers of outside influence on universities and the temptations involved in what he called "the relentless quest for funds." "Federal and state officials give generously to universities," he said. "But the effect has been to make campuses highly dependent on forces beyond our control." He also spoke about the national "fixation on the Harvard mystique," saying,

> However much we protest, I suspect that most of us are secretly pleased to be associated with an institution reputed to have such clout. But we should not forget that these accounts give a distorted picture of what Harvard and other universities actually do or where their true contribution lies.

Bok told his audience that

only education can work simultaneously to develop intellectual capacities, awaken new interests, lift aspirations, provoke important questions, deepen understanding—and these, not the reflected lustre of the institution or the influence of its alumni, must be the university's true contribution to its students.

Derek Bok's speech: It is a great privilege to have all of you in Cambridge for these few days to share our intellectual and cultural life and to celebrate the long, remarkable history of this institution. Many of you have worked to strengthen the University, as your forebears have done since the time of John Harvard and Lady Radcliffe. All of you have enriched us by your presence. To each and every one, I extend our warmest welcome and appreciation.

I always look forward to occasions such as this for the chance they give me to delve again into Harvard history. Nothing could be more therapeutic. No matter what mistakes I make, I invariably find some predecessor who has managed to outdo them. To illustrate, we need only look to the very first year of the College under the reign of my earliest predecessor, Nathaniel Eaton, and his redoubtable bride, Mistress Eaton. Mr. Eaton was barely prevented from beating a teacher to death with a walnut tree plant. Mistress Eaton was accused of putting goat's dung in the hasty pudding. For their sins, they were sacked after only a year of service and the College had to close less than twelve months after it began. Faculty colleagues who grumble about the way they are treated and students who turn up their noses at our cooking should all ponder this episode and put their own complaints in proper historical perspective.

After this modest beginning, Harvard has happily inched forward. Through three and one half centuries, fortunes have been made and unmade, companies have flourished and disappeared, political parties have waxed and waned, yet this venerable institution has persevered, a source of pride to its friends, a cause of apoplexy to its critics but always a force to be reckoned with in American higher education and the country as a whole.

Fifty years have come and gone since we last gathered to celebrate a Harvard anniversary. Looking back on the proceedings then, one is sobered by how few glimmerings there were of the great upheavals that would alter Harvard, the nation, and the entire globe in the decades to come. Scarcely a hint appears of the coming transformation of America's role in the world, the quest for greater opportunity by minority groups and women, the vast changes in health care, or the surging growth of technology that would engulf the nation. Still more significant was the failure to anticipate the mounting importance to America of knowledge itself.

Above all else, it is the centrality of knowledge that had changed the face of Harvard and other universities. Starting, ironically, with the last world war, and continuing with the advances in electronics and biotechnology, the growing sophistication of the professions, the use of policy analysis, and the revolution in modern medicine, we have all become much more aware that in a modern society, knowledge, expertise and new discoveries are the critical ingredients of progress.

Since universities are a principal source of these ingredients, they have come to assume much greater importance than our predecessors could have imagined fifty years ago. Fortunately, American universities have responded to this challenge with remarkable zeal and creativity. Many favoring circumstances helped them to succeed. They were fortunate to escape the destruction of World War II that ravaged higher education in so many other countries. They were enriched by an influx of exceptional scientists and scholars fleeing persecution in Europe. They benefited greatly from the support of the world's most prosperous economy. But most of all, they profited from our distinctive way of organizing higher education.

Throughout our history, universities have enjoyed unusual freedom. Public officials have interfered remarkably little with our state institutions, private groups have found it possible to found their own colleges, and all have engaged in a keen but friendly rivalry for better students, faculty, and facilities. This system is so familiar now that we tend to take it for granted. In fact, it is virtually unique. In almost all other countries, universities are heavily dependent on the government and operate according to the dictates of central planning.

Our free and decentralized system has great strengths. By permitting many independent centers of initiative, it encourages innovation and adaptability. By avoiding state control, it puts the power to make decisions in the hands of those most knowledgeable about education and research. By fostering competition, it generates powerful incentives to excel and improve. The result is a network of universities widely recognized as the finest in the world in the results of their research, the quality of their professional training, their accessibility to a wide spectrum of the population, and the variety of programs they offer to meet the needs of a huge and diverse student population.

There is good reason, then, to regard this as a triumphant moment to celebrate the birth of America's oldest university and of American higher education itself. But ours is an institution with Puritan roots. If there is one characteristic that has marked Harvard through three and a half centuries, it is an abiding sense of unease that causes us to worry even when outward circumstances offer the least excuse for doing so. By instinct, we feel a pang of guilt whenever we catch ourselves enjoying our achievements. We struggle not to mention them out loud . . . with less than total success. We know how often institutions at their zenith bear within them the seeds of eventual decline. For us, therefore, it is second nature to shrink from self-congratulation and to ask ourselves instead what hostile forces, what changes in fortune, what inner contradictions and excesses may come to weaken the modern university and keep it from making the contributions that modern society demands and humankind deserves.

In casting about for sources of concern, we can appropriately begin by looking outside the academy itself. For success and prosperity attract attention, not always of a welcome kind. As universities wax in influence and importance, as their visibility increases and their assets grow, various groups are naturally tempted to use them for purposes of their own choosing.

We have seen much evidence of this in recent years. Military and intelligence agencies have tried to engage professors in secret research and to impose restrictions to keep our scientific findings out of enemy hands. Businesses search for relationships with our scientists that will help them develop new products. Social activists press the university to use its stocks, its purchasing power, its reputation and prestige to fight against apartheid and other evils and injustices. Communities look to our campuses as sources of wealth and leverage to help solve local problems.

In responding to such requests, universities must be keenly aware of their obligation to support the society that sustains them. The question is how they can best contribute and what conditions they must preserve to keep on doing so. All too often, outside groups mistakenly conclude that since the university is successful in teaching and research, it can sway political institutions or solve society's problems as well. Frequently, they press the university to risk its independence by entering into political battles or ask it to act in ways that compromise the openness and freedom that characterize a healthy research environment. In all such cases, the problem is not that people seek the university's help to solve a social problem but that they urge it to act in ways that contradict its proper nature and threaten its most essential functions.

Another concern arising in the outside world is the prospect of excessive government regulation. As knowledge and advanced education become more vital to the society, the state will naturally wish to make sure that institutions supplying these services act according to the public interest. Already, universities are subject to regulations that prohibit discrimination, promote affirmative action, insure accountability for research funds, provide suitable access for the handicapped, and control access to student records, among others.

All these regulations are inspired by the best of motives, and most are perfectly reasonable. The question is how far the process will continue. The Reagan years have given us a temporary respite from further regulation. But plenty of possibilities remain to tempt future administrations: manpower planning to bring the numbers of graduates into line with national needs; reviews of new programs and facilities to avoid duplication and waste; detailed rules to check the abuses of intercollegiate athletics; and safeguards to protect students from unfair grades and arbitrary rejections from the admissions office.

In pondering such regulations, we should clearly acknowledge that universities must be accountable to the public. The dilemma that arises is that adding rules threatens the very qualities that make our universities so successful in serving the public's needs. Higher education in America has thrived on diversity, local autonomy, and competition. Regulation implies uniformity, central planning, and bureaucratic control. The more rules we impose, the more their cumulative weight threatens to transform the environment that has served so well into the kind of system that has seriously hampered our sister institutions abroad.

The prospects for further regulation are connected to a larger problem of worrisome proportions: the ambivalence many people feel toward major research universities as they grow in visibility, influence, and prestige. You have doubtless seen some of the stories about your *alma mater* that have appeared recently in newspapers and magazines. Their photographs are flattering and their tone, by and large, has been friendly and constructive. In reading them, however, you will have noticed a heavy emphasis on the Harvard mystique—our influence in the society, the size of our endowment, the number of our graduates in high places. However much we protest, I suspect that most of us are secretly pleased to be associated with an institution reputed to have such clout. But we should not forget that such accounts give a distorted picture of what Harvard and other universities actually do or where their true contribution lies.

We can all understand this fixation on the Harvard mystique. Aside from the occasional scientific breakthrough, there is not much drama for the reader in the patient labor of scholars surrounded by their books or the quiet growth of mind and feeling that countless students experience. Yet the images that replace these realities are not entirely harmless. As people read of the monetary value of a Harvard diploma, the swelling size of the Harvard endowment, the fabled influence of the old-boy network, fascination and respect easily turn to envy and resentment.

Although these attitudes are not new, the stakes are infinitely greater now that the state plays such a prominent role in financing scientific discovery and student aid. Federal and state officials give generously to universities, recognizing the importance of education and research. But the effect has been to make our campuses highly dependent on forces beyond their control. As a result, Harvard and institutions like it live a much more precarious existence than our predecessors could imagine fifty years ago, and our continued prosperity is much more dependent on the attitudes of the society at large. As we have learned on several occasions in recent years, resentment over the elitism and arrogance of research universities can easily result in hostile treatment at the hands of legislative bodies and executive agencies.

Although the dangers beyond our gates are real enough, it is quite possible that greater hazards will emerge from tensions within our own community. As President Lowell remarked on this occasion in 1936: "If I read history aright institutions have rarely been killed while they were alive. They commit suicide or die from lack of vigor, and then the adversary closes in and buries them." With this warning in mind, we should take careful note of the inner contradictions and pressures that could limit us in carrying out our responsibilities.

In listing the weaknesses of successful institutions it is fashionable to begin by stressing the danger of complacency. And yet, of all our worries, complacency strikes me as the least significant. In my years at Harvard, I have never seen an institution so conscious of the danger of running downhill or so filled with people determined to do creative work. If we are looking for problems, surely there are other concerns that warrant a greater claim on our attention.

One such problem is the difficulty universities experience in setting priorities and limiting growth. This is an understandable failing. As knowledge and expertise grow more important, their uses multiply, and intriguing opportunities constantly appear. Since universities are anarchic by nature and flourish by giving professors free reign, new initiatives continue to blossom, old programs remain, and the institution grows inexorably.

As this process continues, universities become progressively harder to administer. There are so many programs to keep track of, so many appointments to make, so many places where problems can arise, so many activities clamoring for funds that the demands would tax the capacity of even the most experienced manager. Yet experienced management is precisely what universities must do without. By their nature and function, they need to choose their principal officers from the ranks of the faculty. Untrained in the arts of management, these academic leaders are easily overwhelmed by the administrative responsibilities, leaving them little time for the exciting work of conceiving fresh thoughts about the improvement of education and the emerging opportunities for creative research. We may end, therefore, with the worst of both worlds, appointing leaders for their academic experience who have no chance to think about academic questions. This problem has afflicted presidents for some time. Increasingly, it is affecting provosts, deans, and directors of important programs as well.

The constant growth of universities also requires a relentless quest for funds, as many in this audience will be quick to acknowledge. In the increasingly competitive world of higher education, campus representatives must be more and more resourceful in seeking out money from public and private resources. At best, this pressure results in much good-natured pestering. But in big-time athletics, it often leads to a shameless exploitation of athletes. In science, it generates pressures to enter into arrangements with industry or government which contain elements of secrecy or restrictiveness that compromise a free and open environment for investigation. To those of us who labor in the academic vineyard, such methods often seem purified by the noble purposes we seek to achieve. As Bishop Lawrence once said, on setting out to raise money for Harvard: "When you are serving a truly great cause, you cannot afford to be too scrupulous." To skeptics outside the academy, however, who do not share the Bishop's zeal, the scramble for funds often confirms their belief that universities are just another privileged group trying to further its special interests.

Faculty members too are increasingly caught up in the toils of fundraising and administration as they struggle to develop their departments and maintain their research centers. But many professors are encumbered even more by all the opportunities that come to them in a society hungry for expert knowledge. In professional schools and, increasingly, in Arts and Sciences faculties as well, possibilities abound for consulting, government service, going to conferences, and explaining one's field of knowledge to an interested public. Gradually, quietly, these extramural ventures come to represent for many professors a mounting source of excitement, variety, status, and income.

Such activities are not necessarily harmful. They often serve a valuable purpose by bringing professors into contact with interesting people and events that they might otherwise know only vicariously. Still, the activities do take time away from other pursuits more central to the institution's purpose.

These pressures and distractions are unlikely to recede in the next fifty years. On the contrary. Scholars will find it harder to keep up with their field as the volume of knowledge grows constantly greater. Extramural opportunities will increase as society continues to find new needs for expertise. Faculty members will receive more and more requests to help administer the university as it struggles to maintain a larger portfolio of programs and activities.

As the demands increase, how well will we respond? I scarcely know, yet there are surely grounds for concern. In a world where scholars have to specialize so heavily and rely so much on external sources for recognition and support, loyalties are already divided between the university, the profession, and the agencies that supply them funds. As these conflicting pressures grow, and faculties are ever more involved with the society that sustains them, can we expect professors to be immune from the prevailing values of our time? A generation of scholars is coming of age that grew up with Watergate and Vietnam and inherited a pervasive distrust of established institutions. We should not assume that they will feel the same institutional loyalties that their predecessors shared any more than we can count on the same loyalties elsewhere in the society. Instead, in a world that honors success and opulent lifestyles, we could easily find ourselves harboring more and more professors who try to combine the freedom and security of a tenured academic post with the income and visibility tradition- ally reserved for people who take much greater risks and work at much less elevating tasks.

Whether or not these visions materialize, one thing seems cer- tain. In the future, the key ingredient on campus will not be mon- ey, important as it is, but time.

Time does not always work in obvious ways. For example, we know from watching our students carefully that those who try to devote every moment to their studies often lower, rather than raise, their academic performance. The same may be true of scholars as well. People who are engaged in many absorbing tasks bring an intensity to their work that frequently improves its quali- ty. But we also know that there comes a point when extracurricu- lar burdens become so great that academic work begins to suffer. The possibility we confront in future years is that more and more faculty members will go beyond that point.

If they do, what consequences can we expect? Quite possibly, the effects will not be immediately obvious. Scholarly output may not suffer. Lectures may still be competent and informed. But as time for uninterrupted reflection ebbs away, scholarship may in- creasingly lack depth and breadth and rely too much on the work of assistants. There will be less opportunity for the casual contacts with students that may seem unnecessary but often provide the most memorable and critical moments in a young person's life at the university. More likely still, there will be no time to make a serious effort to comprehend how students learn and how they can be helped to learn more. Already, we do not understand enough of what our educational programs accomplish nor do we work systematically enough at finding ways to make them better. We talk a lot about how smart our students are when they enroll, but know too little about how much they learn after they arrive.

Small wonder that outsiders often ignore the true meaning of a university education and describe it in such crass, material terms.

By now, you have heard enough of our concerns to understand what a harvest of problems our successes have brought us. These problems are very different from the challenges that universities surmounted so effectively in the last fifty years. To address today's agenda, we cannot rely on the forces generated by our system of higher education to move us in the right direction, for the hazards I have described are the products of that very system. To prosper in the future, we will have to make a determined effort to resist the pressures that would deflect us from our appointed mission.

In preparing for this task, we will need to keep one thing firmly in mind. All of the dangers I have described share a single characteristic. Each of them results from a failure to appreciate the proper aims of a university and the conditions essential for achieving them. It is easy to ignore these fundamentals. Many of us take them for granted now that we have grown so accustomed to research universities. Some are tempted to push them aside in order to accomplish other ends that seem particularly urgent. At times, we fail to perceive how unfamiliar circumstances threaten our essential values. Whatever the reason, we will need to be much clearer about the functions that universities perform uniquely well and the conditions required to carry them out.

In particular, we will need to persuade the public and to remind ourselves that we are not corporations, not instruments of national security, not militant bodies anxious to force our vision of social justice on the world. Many organizations can offer advice, or help solve society's problems, or develop new products, or further our military aims. But only universities, or institutions like them, can discover the knowledge on which creative solutions rest and only they can educate the men and women who will eventually make the critical decisions. Many individuals can be entrepreneurs, or advocates, or influential advisors. But only scholars blessed with security and freedom can master the largest subjects and pursue the truth wherever the quest may lead them. Many experiences may temper our judgment and help us grow. But only education can work simultaneously to develop intellectual capacities, awaken new interests, lift aspirations, provoke important questions, deepen understanding—and these, not the reflected lustre of the institution or the influence of its alumni, must be the university's true contribution to its students.

To give these values the eloquence they deserve, let me close with another quotation from President Lowell. For if Lowell could not perceive the great events and transformations that lay ahead for Harvard and the future, any more than we can know them today, he surely understood where Harvard's true salvation lay. In his words,

As wave after wave rolls landward from the ocean, breaks and fades away . . . , so the generations of [students] follow one another, sometimes quietly, sometimes, after a storm, with noisy turbulence. But whether we think upon the monotony or the violence in human history, two things are always new—youth and the quest for knowledge, and with these a university is concerned. So long as its interest in them is keen, it can never grow old, though it counts its age by centuries. The means it uses may vary with the times, but forever the end remains the same.

NATIONAL HEALTH PRIORITIES

THE WORSENING CRISIS IN HEALTH CARE[1]
EDWARD M. KENNEDY[2]

During 1986 and 1987, Americans became increasingly aware of two crises in health and medical care. One was the effect of the rapidly escalating cost of medical care on everyone, especially the poor and elderly. The second was the spread of the deadly Acquired Immune Deficiency Syndrome (AIDS). Hardly a day passed that newspapers didn't carry a major report on one or both of these threats, and they were regularly featured in the daily television news.

Senator Edward Kennedy, long an advocate of a comprehensive national health insurance program, addressed the first issue—the growing cost of medical care—in a speech to the American Hospital Association at its annual meeting in Washington, D.C., on February 2, 1987. The speech was delivered to approximately 2,800 members of the American Hospital Association and staffs of various state hospital associations and the AHA at 11:00 A.M. in the International Ballroom of the Washington Hilton Hotel.

Kennedy began his address by associating himself and his message with the audience:

> It's a special pleasure for me to be here today. No cause is closer to my heart than quality health care for every American. And there is no group that cares more about that cause than the administrators and trustees of America's community hospitals. We share a common sense of commitment.

Continuing to identify with his listeners, the senator stated the central thought of his address: "We also share a common sense of urgency because there is a worsening crisis in the ability of millions of Americans to obtain health care that is adequate for their needs and affordable for their pocketbooks."

Kennedy followed a problem-solution pattern in organizing his speech. The problem he addressed is "the shocking lack of access to health care" and the "predictable consequences in human terms" of this lack. The senator observed, "Every American without health insurance is an American tragedy waiting to happen, and it can strike anyone at any age in any community."

He then discussed the possible consequences for infants, children, young parents, middle-aged workers, and senior citizens. Kennedy ex-

---

[1]Delivered to an audience of approximately 2,800 at the annual meeting of the American Hospital Association in the International Ballroom of the Washington Hilton Hotel, Washington, D.C., at 11:00 A.M. on February 2, 1987.

[2]For biographical note, see Appendix.

pressed a special concern for the plight of the elderly, saying that "One of the most pressing problems we face today is the degree to which senior citizens are denied the promise of retirement free from the fear of financial ruin because of illness."

After recommending changes in the insurance programs under Medicare, Kennedy moved to his solution to the problem: "The time has come to require all businesses in America to offer health insurance to all their workers—and all their dependents, too, as a condition of doing business."

Senator Kennedy's speech was part of the American Hospital Association's "Federal Forum," a program which also included speeches by William Roper, Robert Dole, Fortney "Pete" Stark, and Richard Kusserow.

Edward M. Kennedy's speech: It's a special pleasure for me to be here today. No cause is closer to my heart than quality health care for every American. And there is no group that cares more about that cause than the administrators and trustees of America's community hospitals.

We share a common sense of commitment. And we also share a common sense of urgency because there is a worsening crisis in the ability of millions of Americans to obtain health care that is adequate for their needs and affordable for their pocketbooks.

According to the annual count of the Census Bureau, thirty-seven million men, women, and children have no health insurance coverage at all. For 15 million more, the coverage is inadequate by any realistic standard. Since 1980, the number of uninsured Americans has risen by more than a million citizens each year.

Partly, the problem stems from the chronic high unemployment in our society and the changing nature of the work force—the shift from heavy manufacturing jobs to service sector jobs, where health insurance coverage has traditionally been absent.

Partly, it stems from the failure of benefits under AFDC and Medicaid to keep pace with continuing inflation. And partly it flows from harsh recent changes in federal welfare rules, changes instigated by an administration that is no friend of the needy, and that make it impossible for many of the working poor to qualify for Medicaid.

The shocking lack of access to health care has predictable consequences in human terms. Every American without health insurance is an American tragedy waiting to happen, and it can strike anyone at any age in any community.

Infants will die at birth or suffer lifetimes of pain or disability because their mothers did not receive even minimal prenatal health care. Decent prenatal care should be the birthright of every newborn infant in America, and I intend to do all I can to see that this Congress guarantees that right.

What of the children, who will lose the precious chance for a healthy start in the early years of life, because they never see a doctor? Often, physical and mental disabilities can be corrected if caught in time. And they can be diagnosed at routine childhood screenings that also ought to be available to every American child.

What of young parents, whose hopes for the future will be dashed when sudden serious illness saddles them with Everests of debt?

What of middle-aged workers, who will lose a lifetime in savings and security for their retirement years?

And what of the senior citizens, who built this country and made it great? They must not become forgotten Americans when they fall victim to catastrophic illness or seek long-term nursing care.

As hospital administrators and trustees, you live with these daily human tragedies. One of the noblest missions of your institutions is to provide care to every member of the community, regardless of ability to pay. For generations, the willingness of voluntary hospitals to care for the indigent has represented America at its best. But all of you know that this historic mission of mercy is being overwhelmed today by rising costs and rising need.

The highly competitive health care market is forcing hospitals to offer care at the lowest possible price, with little room for surcharges to subsidize the poor. But without that well-intentioned padding, charity care will fail. "Free care" cannot pass the truth-in-labelling test, because it is a service that someone has to pay for.

There is no free lunch in health care or in life, and the sooner the Reagan administration accepts that truth, the sooner we will roll up our sleeves together and tackle the problem of vanishing charity care for the needy. No hospital in America should face the cruel choice between bankrupting itself or barring its doors to those who cannot pay.

It is an unfortunate truth that federal and state reimbursement policies are now making this problem worse. I am a strong supporter of prospective payment for hospital services. But I do not support a policy that year after year ratchets the reimbursement down. We need a balanced and well-considered policy on health care spending, not a meat-ax approach that sees only the budget deficit.

America's hospitals did not cause the federal deficit; they cannot cure it; and a budget policy that turns hospitals into cannon fodder in the war against the deficit is as irresponsible as it is counter-productive. Nor should federal policy toward hospital capital investment be driven by a misplaced desire to implement an economic pipe dream, especially when that pipe dream means a nightmare for every hospital that has renovated its facilities or needs to renovate them in the future.

One of the most pressing problems we face today is the degree to which senior citizens are denied the promise of a retirement free from the fear of financial ruin because of illness.

Medicare ranks second only to Social Security among the greatest triumphs of social policy for the elderly in the past half century. But unlike Social Security, we have permitted Medicare to fall behind in the struggle to keep pace with modern need. Two decades after its enactment, Medicare covers less than half the health care costs of senior citizens. Listen to the litany of gaps. Medicare offers no protection against lengthy hospital stays. Medicare demands an exorbitantly high deductible before a patient is even permitted to pass through the hospital door. Medicare has no limit on costs for physician services. Medicare does not cover out-patient drugs, even for victims of chronic illness. And if Medicare does not cover these essential costs, who will?

I am not here to bash the private sector or to criticize the private health insurance industry for failing to bail out Medicare. In many respects, the industry has done an excellent job in holding the line while government has been abdicating its responsibility.

We enacted Medicare twenty-two years ago to meet precisely the problem we face today. We understood that privatization of health insurance means povertization of the elderly. But Medicare today is not doing the job it should, and Medigap cannot fill the gap alone. Senior citizens with private insurance pay markups for administrative costs of ten to forty percent of their premium dollar, and often even more. If that same protection were provided by Medicare, the administrative cost would be less than two percent, and billions of dollars would be saved.

Secretary Otis Bowen has proposed to meet a major portion of this need by offering senior citizens a catastrophic insurance program under Medicare. That program is obviously overdue—and it is sad to see the Reagan Administration scratching so hard for ways to escape the Bowen plan.

But it is heartening to see the broad bipartisan support already generated in Congress and across the country for this sensible, simple proposal by a physician from the heartland of America who is also a member of the Reagan Cabinet. In the end, Donald Regan may not like Doc Bowen's plan, but I suspect that Ronald Reagan will. $4.92 a month is not too much to pay for elderly peace of mind. The issue is not whether a bill will pass, but whether and by how much Congress will improve upon the Bowen plan.

I have already introduced legislation to implement the plan, and so have others. As these measures move through Congress, I am convinced that we can make Medicare do more, especially in critical areas such as out-patient drugs, out-patient psychiatric services, the special needs of the low income elderly and the homeless elderly and, if possible, the massive need for help that millions of senior citizens face in obtaining long-term nursing care.

I hope that this new momentum on Medicare will carry over into other health care needs. But for millions of non-elderly Americans who are uninsured and the millions more who are under-insured, the commitment of Congress and the President is in doubt. The vast majority of uninsured Americans are not freeloaders. Three-quarters are workers or their dependents. Most of them work 40 hours or more a week, fifty-two weeks a year. The reason they have no health insurance is that their employers don't provide it.

The time has come to require all businesses in America to offer health insurance to all their workers—and all their dependents, too—as a condition of doing business. Employers have been required by law since 1938 to pay a minimum wage, and in 1987 it is time to insist that they provide at least a minimum health insurance, too.

A minimum benefit package does not mean Cadillac plans or first dollar coverage of health expenses. It does mean basic coverage of hospital and physician bills, and it also means protection against catastrophic costs. No American worker should have the fear of serious illness compounded by the fear of financial ruin.

Three-quarters of workers without insurance have jobs in firms with 25 employees or less. I am aware of the additional burden a program of this type may place on small business. But there are ways to minimize the burden.

When each small firm must negotiate a separate insurance package, the costs are high. When small businesses purchase health insurance for small groups of workers, they pay up to 40 percent more than large firms for identical coverage. For individual workers who seek individual plans, the expense is often out of reach, and impossible to purchase at any price for those whose health is poor. Many employees play Russian roulette with their own and their family's health, because food and shelter and clothing are more pressing daily needs.

By pooling insurance costs in appropriate geographical areas, we can bring the burden on individual businesses down. By ending the discrimination against small firms in the tax laws, we can achieve additional reductions in the burden. And by doing so, we will actually cut costs for all the small businesses in America that do the decent thing and already insure their workers.

In spite of the ideological alarms you may be hearing from some quarters, the minimum health care law I favor is not at war with our current health care system. It is not back-door national health insurance any more than the minimum wage is back-door wage and price control.

A minimum health care law creates no burdensome regulations for health providers. It requires no massive bureaucracy. It simply extends the current system of employment-based private health insurance to millions of workers denied it now. And it will benefit thousands of community hospitals who will no longer have to fear that the patient at the door cannot pay for the bed the hospital will provide.

Modest and basic as this proposal is, powerful forces are already aligning themselves against it. To those who argue that the additional cost will damage America's competitive position in the world, I reply: the businesses at the cutting edge of competition already provide health insurance for their workers. They should not have to pay billions of dollars in hospital charges for other people's uncovered workers.

So let us tell the truth about who really pays for the uninsured. It is time to place these costs where they belong: on the shoulders of the relatively small numbers of firms who refuse to protect their workers. And if we succeed in this endeavor, the country as a whole will be the winner, because a healthier America is also a more competitive America.

To those who see this proposal as an unwarranted intrusion by big government, I say that for half a century, government has required businesses to pay minimum wages, provide unemployment compensation, and participate in Social Security.

It violates no legitimate notion of the proper role of government—and it does not breach any proper wall of separation between the public and private sector—for Congress to fulfill the constitutional concept of promoting the general welfare by providing health insurance to those who work.

Our opponents are already crying wolf about the welfare state and the road to socialized medicine. But I say, the principle is clear, the precedents are there, and it is time for Congress to act.

This proposal should be passed in the 100th Congress, and it can be passed in the 100th Congress. But it will only be passed if all of you here today join in the effort to enact it.

America can never repay the debt it owes to the American Hospital Association for the extraordinary contributions you have made to health policy and health progress in the past. Now, a new challenge awaits us in the months ahead. A new partnership and a new Congress summon us to act. And for you and for the American health care system, may the best be yet to come.

EDUCATING OUR CHILDREN ABOUT AIDS[1]
C. Everett Koop[2]

By March 1987, more than 32,000 Americans had been diagnosed as having AIDS (Acquired Immune Deficiency Syndrome), and nearly 60 percent of them had died. Medical experts warned that the epidemic, first diagnosed in 1981, had only just begun. Government scientists projected that

. . . by the end of 1991, the total number of cases will reach 270,000, with 179,000 deaths unless better treatments are found. In

---

[1]Delivered to the Mayors' AIDS Task Force at the annual midwinter meeting of the United States Conference of Mayors at the Capitol Hilton Hotel in Washington, D.C., on January 23, 1987, at 1:00 P.M.
[2]For biographical note, see Appendix.

the year 1991 alone, some 54,000 Americans are expected to die of acquired immune deficiency syndrome, an annual loss comparable to the death toll of the entire Vietnam War. (Erik Eckholm, *New York Times*, March 16, 1987, p. 11)

Initially, the disease had surfaced in this country in major cities and affected mostly homosexuals and users of illegal intravenous drugs, but by 1987 it had spread to every state and was appearing among increasing numbers of heterosexuals, both male and female. Health officials estimated that up to one and a half million Americans carried the AIDS virus in their bodies and that perhaps one-fourth of them would develop AIDS within five years of their infection.

As public concern grew, a debate over how to control the disease began to emerge. Since no effective cure or treatment was available, the debate was on how best to prevent its spread. The three main factions were: (1) those who believed that courses should be taught in the public schools from an early grade which included explicit instruction on sexual relations and specific information on the use of contraceptives; (2) those who believed that the schools should teach about sex only as a part of marriage, stressing premarital abstinence and chastity; and (3) those who argued that sexual attitudes, morality, and religion are intertwined and in no way are the responsibility of the government or the public schools.

In this controversy, the best known and most unlikely spokesman for a program of explicit sex education in the schools was the Surgeon General of the United States, Dr. C. Everett Koop. At the time of his appointment, Koop—a "born again" evangelical Christian—was regarded as a "right winger" and opponent of abortion. Following his outspokenness on the AIDS issue, liberals who had once criticized the Surgeon General as "scary" praised him as "a man of heroic proportions." On the other side, conservatives who had pushed for Koop's confirmation six years earlier regarded him as having "failed in moral courage."

> The doctor has become a lightning rod for one of the most sensitive moral issues in the country: How do you talk about sex in a way that is explicit enough to give health information without seeming to condone certain practices? . . . Dr. Koop fiercely wants to strip AIDS of its stigma and stop people from dying. To that end, he talks boldly about the proper way to use condoms. (*New York Times*, April 6, 1987, p. 14)

Gay rights leaders came to regard Koop as a hero, albeit an unlikely one, at a time when "we really needed him."

The Surgeon General said that he had not changed; it was just that people had come to know him better, explaining:

> As you mature in any kind of situation, you become more understanding about it. . . . I hate injustice of any kind and I don't like to see people excoriated in the midst of illness because there's some other part of their life-style that people don't like. . . . If a policeman and a bandit are hurt in a crime shootout and brought into the emergency room, I don't ignore the bandit and take care of the cop. I take care of the one who needs help the most. . . . I guess what

I'd like people to say about me, when the controversy dies down, is that I handled the job with integrity and didn't bow to pressures. (Maureen Dowd, *New York Times,* April 4, 1987, p. 14)

Surgeon General Koop delivered the following speech to the Mayors' AIDS Task Force at the annual midwinter meeting of the United States Conference of Mayors at the Capitol Hilton Hotel in Washington, D.C., on January 23, 1987, at 1:00 P.M., to an audience of approximately 100 mayors, local health officers, city staff, and press representatives. Dr. Koop spoke as one member of a panel that also included San Francisco Mayor Dianne Feinstein, Dr. James Curran of the Center for Disease Control, and Dr. David Wedegar of the San Francisco Health Commission. The speech received widespread publicity, including coverage by the *New York Times, Washington Post,* NBC news, and several syndicated columnists.

By coincidence, on the same day that Koop was advocating explicit sex education courses in the schools, United States Secretary of Education William J. Bennett delivered an address opposing this kind of training and endorsing instead instruction stressing moral values and sexual abstinence. (See pp. 58-70.) The two Reagan administration officials again contradicted each other—again coincidentally on the same day—when on May 1 Bennett delivered a speech in which he advocated mandatory AIDS testing for hospital patients, couples engaged to be married, prisoners, and immigrants while Koop opposes mandatory testing, arguing that the tests would cause those vulnerable to the deadly disease "to go underground."

C. Everett Koop's speech: I'm pleased to have the chance to speak to this group of key government officials. Over the past couple of months, ever since I released *The Surgeon General's Report on AIDS,* I've felt that my office—of any office I know—is "where the action is." But in my more sober moments, I have to admit that each one of you has the "action" in our country. I can produce a report on AIDS and have it be a good one—and I truly believe it is—but the people who actually have AIDS are in your cities. They're your constituents, and they look to you and to your colleagues in local public health agencies for the help they need. I know that. And so, I'm pleased to talk with you and, if possible, offer you some insight into what this problem is all about.

First of all, as you know, our experience with AIDS is only six years old. The first reports of the disease were sent from some of your cities into our Centers for Disease Control in Atlanta in June, 1981. You already know the rest of the history of the disease since then, so I won't go into it.

I want to emphasize, however, that we're talking about a disease that's spreading. The number of victims is doubling in little more than a year. For example, as of January 1986, we had a cumulative total of 16,000 reported cases. Today that cumulative total is 30,000, and over half of them have already died of the disease. And the rest apparently will.

Last year we had over 13,000 new cases added to the total. This year we expect another 23,000 new cases. By the end of 1990 a quarter of a million people will have contracted AIDS. Make no mistake about it. AIDS is spreading among more people, and it is fatal.

Now, even though scientists have had a look at the AIDS virus itself, we don't really know what it is, and unless we know that, we have no way of permanently stopping it. Yes, we're making progress in the research effort, but it's very slow going.

People ask, "When will we have an effective vaccine available?" And I have to tell them that I don't see one in the foreseeable future. I will remind you that it took 19 years to develop the hepatitis B vaccine, and that was a comparatively easy virus to understand.

There are a lot of things we don't know about AIDS. But we do know with complete certainty that the AIDS virus is transmitted from one person to another either in blood or in semen. It's a peculiar trait of a virus, I'll admit. But there it is.

And while it may be peculiar, it is also the most serious piece of information we have. It explained, for example, why AIDS has been so prevalent among homosexual and bisexual men. Some homosexual sex practices not only produce semen but they also cause some bleeding.

The second largest group of AIDS carriers are drug abusers who borrow dirty intravenous needles from other addicts who already have AIDS.

When we first began to confront the AIDS epidemic, the people at highest risk were homosexual and bisexual men. I'm afraid they still are, even though homosexuals have apparently become much more cautious about their sexual practices. This is clear from the downward trend-lines of other diseases, such as gonorrhea, herpes, and syphilis, in the gay community. However, the virus has a long incubation period and many men who are more cautious today and show no signs of the disease are nevertheless carrying the virus in their bloodstreams.

Make no mistake about this: homosexual and bisexual men are still the primary high-risk group, and they are also the primary group transmitting the disease as well. But lately we've been seeing a rise in the reports of AIDS occurring among heterosexual men and women who are not I.V. drug abusers. In fact, their heterosexual activity seems to be their only risk factor. As of last week, about 4 percent of all AIDS reports involved heterosexual men and women. That's not much. However, while we anticipate that the overall numbers of AIDS cases will increase about 9-fold over the next five years, the number of AIDS cases involving heterosexuals will increase about 20-fold.

So far, we've beamed virtually all our information and education efforts at homosexual and bisexual men. But now that the disease is occurring more and more among heterosexual men and women, we need to direct our information and education efforts out to the whole society, which, of course, is predominantly heterosexual. This new development also means that the geography of this disease is changing. At one time we were concerned primarily—almost exclusively—with the homosexual communities in San Francisco, Los Angeles, and New York City, and these are still the cities with the highest numbers of AIDS cases.

But they're no longer alone. Other cities and states are showing a rise in cases, too. You've probably heard some of these figures already, but let me offer just a couple: Houston had 77 cases in 1983, but it reported 345 last year; Dallas had only 26 AIDS cases in 1983—it had 208 last year; Atlanta had 25 in 1983—it had 185 last year; Boston had 38 in 1983 and 155 last year.

Now, for the benefit of some people here from state capitols, let me add these figures: Colorado reported 167 new cases during 1986, but only 63 new cases in 1985; Ohio had 173 new ones last year, but only 64 a year ago; and Arkansas had 40 new cases last year, but only 27 in all of 1985.

These broadly geographic trend-lines were already appearing, when President Reagan asked me—back in February of 1986—to pull together everything we knew about AIDS and put it in a plain-English report to the American people.

I met with individuals and groups from across the spectrum of society: groups like the National Education Association and the National P.T.A.; the Christian Life Commission of the Southern Baptist Convention and the Synagogue Council of America; with the National Coalition of Black and Lesbian Gays and the Washington Business Group on Health. I had good meetings with the representatives of local, county, and state and territorial health officials, also, 26 groups in all. They were extraordinarily helpful, and each one pledged to do whatever was necessary to distribute my report across the length and breadth of America.

After 8 months of listening and writing, I delivered my report to the White House. Late last September the cabinet heard it and accepted it, the Domestic Policy Council heard and accepted it, and, of course, the President accepted it. I want to assure you that at no time did anyone suggest a little change here and a little something there. I'm happy to say that the final published report I released on October 22 was the exact same report that I personally wrote between February and September of last year.

I think the report has done two things: First, it has impressed the country generally that AIDS was indeed everybody's problem. We had said that before, but nobody really wanted to believe it. Now they must.

Second, the report makes it clear that we have to stop the disease not by waiting around for the development of a vaccine but by teaching our young people the facts about AIDS and—hopefully—thereby ending the chain of transmission once and for all with the help of a new generation of enlightened, cautious Americans. Heterosexual as well as homosexual young people are now at high risk. How they live out their sexuality over a long period of time will determine whether our society can survive this devastating disease or not. And this is the difficult part. What we have to do over the next several years is educate and inform young people about AIDS, about their own sexuality in such a way that they can become a little more responsible than their elders have been.

I know you're all wondering what educational messages you should plan in your communities. I won't be prescriptive, but let me offer a couple of suggestions.

The first one is simple enough: It's monogamy. In other words, short of total abstinence, the best defense against AIDS is to maintain a faithful, monogamous relationship, the kind of relationship in which you have only one continuing sexual partner, and that person is as faithful as you are. This may sound like a morality lesson, but it also happens to be good science. In containing the epidemic of AIDS, science and morality walk hand-in-hand toward the same goal.

My second message is for people who don't yet have a faithful monogamous relationship for whatever reason. My message is caution. You need to know with absolute certainty that neither

you nor your partner is carrying the AIDS virus. If you are not absolutely certain, then you must take precautions. In such situations I advise the following:
• Don't have sex with someone who already has AIDS. Period.
• Don't have sex with someone who could carry the virus of AIDS, a person who, for example, practices high-risk behavior. That includes homosexuals, intravenous drug users, prostitutes, and other persons who have many different sex partners. Obviously the same message goes to any of those high-risk individuals.
• And finally, if you do decide to have sex with such an individual anyway—a decision that could have serious health consequences—then, if you're a man, at least use a condom from start to finish. If you're a woman, make sure your male partner uses a condom. A condom won't provide 100 percent protection—few things in life do—but so far it seems to be the best protection short of monogamy.

If sexually active people will heed these two messages, they will achieve a high degree of protection and will most likely not be infected with the AIDS virus.

What else can we do to combat this terrible disease?

In my report on AIDS, I also advise people to avoid those sex practices which can cause cuts or tears in the linings of the rectum, vagina, or penis. I say, don't have sex with female or male prostitutes. I strongly advise young people to stay clear of drugs and alcohol, because these substances lower your ability to think clearly and protect yourself from danger, especially the danger of having sex with an AIDS-infected partner.

And I also suggest that we educate our young people about AIDS and about sexuality. Young people are curious and eager for such knowledge. They're still learning about their bodies and their emotions, they're still unsure about their own sexuality, and they still have that priceless optimism about the world and the people in it. I prefer to speak about the need for "AIDS education," and I truly believe we need such education at the appropriate age level in the schools of America.

But I also recognize that, for many young people, such education may be frightening, or puzzling, or both. Hence, I believe that the most significant action our society might take to protect its young people from the mortal threat of AIDS is to provide them with education concerning their own sexuality that is factually correct, personally sensitive, and morally strong.

The term "sex education" is one I'm not at all comfortable with because it immediately polarizes any audience. Also, in my view, "sex education" usually means a course of instruction that is much too limited. Let me explain what I mean by that.

Most of the time, when you hear the phrase, "sex education," you think of class time devoted to human reproductive biology, including carefully phrased explanations about the use and abuse of the male and female genitalia. I'm told that young people call these classes "organ recitals."

Most schools now offer this minimum kind of sex education some time during the junior high or middle school years and that's a good thing, although it might be a little late. I personally would urge that the material be presented earlier, among 9-, 10-, and 11-year-olds.

Of course, developmental age is more important than chronological age. Also, community standards, which vary from place to place, must be taken into account. Grade-school children are extremely curious about themselves. They are also kinder and more generous than older children, or even most adults, for that matter. And they are, above all, susceptible to being loved and to offering much love in return. And sex education without the concept of love and responsibility is like a piece of pie that's all crust and no filling.

My own preference, therefore, would be to have our elementary schools introduce children to the subject of reproductive biology within a more general discussion of the nature of sensitive and affirmative human relations. That's easier to say than to do, I know. And furthermore, some parents get uneasy about having the schools impart certain human values to their children. They think that such instruction should be done at home.

And I agree. My advice to parents has always been the same: the social and spiritual development of your children is your business. Don't pass it up, don't pass it by, pass it on. Parents agree with me 100 percent. But most of them, I have to confess, never do much more than agree with me. Nevertheless, I encourage parents to talk openly, clearly, and affirmatively with young people about their developing physiology. But I want them to give some other information, too.

As I indicated earlier, "sex education" means more to me than just an "organ recital." "Sex education" ought to deal with relationships between men and women that are loving, caring, respectful, and tolerant. Such relationships include some fulfilling sexual activity, but they are not defined only by that activity. There's much more to human relationships than just "good sex." And young people ought to be advised of that.

But for many people, such a balanced relationship is an ideal. "Real life" isn't always like that. Grown-ups know about human imperfection. But children don't. And grown-ups can deal with human imperfection. But children can't unless we help them. Without a compassionate understanding of the imperfect nature of many human relationships, a child's education will be, itself, very imperfect.

So if parents are to educate their children about human relationships—sexual and otherwise—they must first understand and accept the nature of their own. For many of us, that's hard to do. And then they must be able to tell their children about that relationship. I'd like parents to do this with compassion, with respect and love, and with some understanding not just of the child who is listening, but also of the adult who is speaking. And that's even harder to do.

I'm sharing these thoughts with you today because I want you to know that my deepest wish is still for the parents of this country to be the primary teachers of sex and human relations to their children. And I say that, knowing full well that this may be an assignment that some parents simply can't handle. When that's the case, then I believe there is a compelling social need for our schools, churches, synagogues, and other communal institutions—including our local governments—to do whatever they can to provide our children with the most helpful kinds of information.

Our children don't live in a vacuum, as we all know. They live in a real world of pleasure and danger, along with the rest of us. But we have some experience with it and some sense of how to survive in it, with our lives and our values intact. And I believe, therefore, that each of us—in our homes or in our schools—has the moral responsibility to pass that information on to our children. We can't leave it by default to the movies, television, or the street-corner. Not if you value the young lives that are now at stake.

This has been a grim message, and I guess I am a grim courier. I only hope that everyone who hears it or reads it will also believe it and do his or her part to stop the spread of AIDS, protect and save the lives of people at risk, including unsuspecting young people, and return human sexuality back to its rightful place: part of the total complex of human, caring interpersonal relations.

SEX AND THE EDUCATION OF OUR CHILDREN[1]
WILLIAM J. BENNETT[2]

"William J. Bennett is a hard man to ignore," wrote reporter Robin Wilson, noting the seemingly ubiquitous media presence of the current Secretary of Education.

> Flip the television on to *Meet the Press* or the *MacNeil/Lehrer NewsHour* and the controversial Secretary of Education is likely to be telling interviewers about his latest cause. Pick up a newspaper or news magazine and he's probably quoted in at least one article or is the subject of an editorial.
> Mr. Bennett made three television appearances last month, had interviews with seven journalists, and held press conferences after almost every speech delivered. . . . He is one of the most visible members of President Reagan's Cabinet and has received far more press attention than his predecessors. (*Chronicle of Higher Education*, December 10, 1986, p. 16)

Some critics have called Bennett a "media hound" more concerned with how much news coverage he gets about a speech than with the substance of the address itself. Other people say he is merely using the press to bring education issues to the forefront. Bennett himself claims, "I want to have a conversation with the American people about education, and I can't hold those conversations individually, so the media is the way I get to make my points publicly." (*Chronicle of Higher Education*, December 10, 1986, p. 17)

Whatever his motives, the Secretary of Education made headlines when on the same day that Surgeon General C. Everett Koop endorsed a program of explicit sex education in the schools for children as young as 9, 10, and 11 (see speech, pp. 49-58), Bennett spoke out against Koop's proposal, arguing that AIDS education should be "value-based" and aimed at teaching abstinence as the key to protection. In his address at the National School Board Association's conference on "Building Character in Public Schools" in Washington, D.C., on January 23, 1987, Bennett lashed out at a recent National Academy of Sciences report which called for making contraceptives "available to all teenagers at low or no cost."

The speech received widespread coverage in the national press and

---

[1]Delivered to the National School Board Association's conference on "Building Character in Public Schools" in Washington, D.C. at the Hyatt Regency Capitol Hill Hotel on January 22, 1987.
[2]For biographical note, see Appendix.

was the subject of special features by the Associated Press, the Educational Services Department, and several syndicated columnists. Reaction to
the speech was divided. The president of the National School Board Association, Nellie C. Weil, said she welcomed Bennett's emphasis on character, but felt he was "wrong in assuming the public schools are not teaching
the rightness and wrongness of things." Faye Wattleton, president of the
Planned Parenthood Federation, said that parents, not schools, should
teach children to abstain from sex. She called Bennett's speech "politically
inspired" and fodder for "the anti-sex-education elements in this
country." But some educators, including the California Superintendent
of Public Instruction, welcomed Bennett's emphasis on character-
building as a key element in any sex education course. (Associated Press,
Baton Rouge *State Times*, January 23, 1987, p. 4A)

According to Leslie Maitland Werner, the disagreement between Surgeon General Koop and Secretary of Education Bennett had been the
subject of at least two meetings of the Reagan administration's Domestic
Policy Council (*New York Times*, January 24, 1987, p. 7) About a month
after Werner's report, President Reagan seemed to have decided in favor
of Bennett's position when he endorsed a campaign to educate the public
about the dangers of AIDS, but only if the campaign stressed "responsible
sexual behavior" within marriage and taught sexual abstinence. (Philip M.
Boffey, *New York Times*, February 26, 1987, p. 10)

William J. Bennett's speech: I've spent a good deal of my time as
Secretary of Education talking about character. I've said that
schools, teachers, and principals must help develop good character. I've said that they don't have to reinvent the wheel, we don't
have to add special courses or devise new materials for the purpose of instilling character in the young. There is no great mystery or trick to this task: parents and teachers have been doing
it for centuries. We simply need to put students in the presence
of adults of sound character, adults who know the difference between right and wrong, who will articulate it to children, who will
remind them of the human experience with that difference, and
who will live that difference in front of them. Aristotle gave us
this prescription more than two thousand years ago: In order to
teach good character, expose children to good character and in-
vite its imitation. It has been the experience of mankind, confirmed by the findings of contemporary psychology, that this
prescription works, that it still works.

Today I would like to talk about one place in which attention
must be paid to character in an explicit, focused way. That is in
the classroom devoted to sex education. It would be undesirable,
but a teacher could conduct large portions of a class in English
or history without explicit reference to questions of character.
But to neglect questions of character in a sex education class

would be a great and unforgivable error. Sex education has to do with how boys and girls, how men and women, treat each other and themselves. It has to do with how boys and girls, how men and women, *should* treat each other and themselves. Sex education is therefore about character and the formation of character. A sex education course in which issues of right and wrong do not occupy center stage is an evasion and an irresponsibility.

Sex education is much in the news. Many states and localities are considering proposals to implement or expand sex education curricula. I understand the reasons why such proposals are under consideration. And indeed, polls suggest that a substantial majority of the American people favor sex education in the schools. I too tend to support the idea. It seems reasonable to the American people, and to me, for the schools to provide another opportunity for students to become both more knowledgeable and more thoughtful about this important area of life. To have such matters treated well by adults whom students and their parents trust would be a great improvement on the sex curriculum available on the street and on television.

For several years now, though, I have been looking at the actual form the idea of sex education assumes once it is in the classroom. Having surveyed samples of the literature available to the schools, and having gained a sense of the attitudes that pervade some of this literature, I must say this: I have my doubts. It is clear to me that some programs of sex education are not constructive. In fact, they may be just the opposite. In some places, some people, to be sure, are doing an admirable job. But in all too many places, sex education classes are failing to give the American people what they are entitled to expect for their children, and what their children deserve.

Seventy percent of all high school seniors had taken sex education courses in 1985, up from 60 percent in 1976. Yet when we look at what is happening in the sexual lives of American students, we can only conclude that it is doubtful that much sex education is doing any good at all. The statistics by which we may measure how our children, how our boys and girls, are treating one another sexually are little short of staggering:

More than one-half of America's young people have had sexual intercourse by the time they are 17.

More than one million teenage girls in the United States become pregnant each year. Of those who give birth, nearly half are not yet 18.

Teen pregnancy rates are at or near an all-time high. A 25 percent decline in birth rates between 1970 and 1984 is due to a *doubling* of the abortion rate during that period. More than 400,000 teenage girls now have abortions each year.

Unwed teenage births rose 200 percent between 1960 and 1980.

Forty percent of today's 14-year-old girls will become pregnant by the time they are 19.

These numbers are, I believe, an irrefutable indictment of sex education's effectiveness in reducing teenage sexual activity and pregnancies. For these numbers have grown even as sex education has expanded. I do *not* suggest that sex education has *caused* the increase in sexual activity among youth; but clearly it has not prevented it. As Larry Cuban, professor of education at Stanford University, has written, "Decade after decade . . . statistics have demonstrated the ineffectiveness of such courses in reducing sexual activity [and] teenage pregnancy. . . . In the arsenal of weapons to combat teenage pregnancy, school-based programs are but a bent arrow. However, bent arrows do offer the illusion of action."

Why do many sex education courses offer merely the illusion of action? When one examines the literature and materials available to the schools, one often discovers in them a certain pervasive tone, a certain attitude. That attitude is this. Offer students technical information, offer the facts, tell them they have choices, and tell them what the consequences of those choices could be, *but do no more*. And there is the problem.

Let me give you a few examples. And let me say that these are not "worst case" examples, that is, they are not examples of the most controversial and provocative material used in some sex education courses. These are, rather, examples of approaches commonly used in many schools.

A curriculum guide for one of the largest school systems in the country suggests strategies to "help students learn about their own attitudes and behaviors and find new ways of dealing with problems." For example, students are given the following so-called "problem situation," asked to "improvise dialogue" and "act it out," and then discuss "how everyone felt about the interactions."

Susan and Jim are married. He becomes intoxicated and has sex with his secretary. He contracts herpes, but fails to tell Susan.

What will happen in this situation?
How would you react if you were Susan and found out?

The so-called "Expected Outcome" of this exercise of "acting out" and "interacting" is to get the student "to recognize sexually transmitted diseases as a threat to the individual."

Another lesson presents a situation of an unmarried girl who has become pregnant. Various parties in her life recommend various courses of action, from marriage to adoption to abortion. Having described the situation, the teacher is then supposed to ask the following questions:

Which solution do you like best? Why?
Which solution do you like least? Why?
What would you do if you were in this situation?

And the "Expected Outcome" of this exercise is "to identify alternative actions for an unintended pregnancy." Now we know what will likely happen in the classroom discussion of this lesson. Someone will opt for one course of action, others will raise their hands and argue for something else, more will speak, the teacher will listen to all opinions, and that will be that. The teacher will move on, perhaps saying the discussion was good, that students should be talking about this, and that as long as they are talking about it, even if they do not arrive at a clear position, they are somehow being educated.

Now the point I would like to make is that exercises like these deal with very complex, sensitive, personal, serious, and often agitated situations, situations that involve human beings at their deepest levels. But the guiding pedagogical instruction to teachers in approaching all such "Sensitive and Personal Issues" is this, and I quote: "Where strong differences of opinion exist on what is right or wrong sexual behavior, objective, informed and dignified discussion of both sides of such questions should be encouraged." And that's it—no more. The curriculum guide is loaded with devices to help students "explore the options," "evaluate the choices involved," "identify alternative actions," and "examine their own values." It provides some facts for students, some definitions, some information, lots of "options," but that's all.

What's wrong with this kind of teaching? First, it is a very odd king of teaching, very odd because it does not teach. It does not teach because, while speaking to a very important aspect of human life, it displays a conscious aversion to making moral distinctions. Indeed, it insists on holding them in abeyance. The words of morality, of a rational, mature morality, seem to have been banished from this sort of sex education.

To do what is being done in these classes is tantamount to throwing up our hands and saying to our young people, "We give up. We give up. We give up on teaching right and wrong to you. Here, take these facts, take this information, and take your feelings, your options, and try to make the best decisions you can. But you're on your own. We can say no more." It is ironic that, in the part of our children's lives where they may most need adult guidance, and where indeed I believe they most want it, too often the young find instead an abdication of responsible moral authority.

Now I ask this: Do we or do we not think that sex for children is serious business, entailing serious consequences? If we do, then we need to be more than neutral about it in front of our children. When adults maintain a studiously value-neutral stance, the impression likely to be left is that, in the words of one twelfth-grader, "No one says not to do it, and by default they're condoning it." And a sex education curriculum that simply provides options, and condones by default, is not what the American people want, nor is it what our children deserve.

It is not that the materials used in most of our schools are urging students to go out and have sexual intercourse. In fact, they give reasons why students might want to choose not to have intercourse, and they try to make students "comfortable" with that decision. Indeed, you sometimes get the feeling that, for these guides, being "comfortable" with one's decision, with exercising one's "option," is the sum and substance of the responsible life. Decisions aren't right or wrong, decisions simply make you comfortable or not. It is as though "comfort" alone had now become our moral compass. These materials are silent as to any other moral standards, any other standards of right and wrong, by which a student might reach a decision to refrain from sex and which would give him or her the inner resources to stick by it.

It seems to me, then, if this is how sex education goes, that we should not wonder at its failure to stem the rising incidence of teenage sex, teenage pregnancies, teenage abortions, and single teenaged parents. One developer of a sex education curriculum recently said, "If you measure success in terms of reduction of teen pregnancy, I don't know if it has been successful. But in terms of orientation and preparation for students to comfortably incorporate sexuality into their lives, it has been helpful." There's that telltale "comfortable." But American parents expect more than that from their schools. Americans consistently say that they want our schools to provide reliable standards of right and wrong to guide students through life. In short, I think most Americans want to urge not what might be the "comfortable" thing, but the right thing. Why are we so afraid to say what that is?

I believe the American people expect from sex education courses in the schools that their children will be taught the basic information, the relevant biology, the relevant physiology, what used to be called the "facts of life." But they also expect that those facts will be placed in a moral context. In a recent national poll, 70 percent of the adults surveyed said they thought sex education programs should teach moral values, and about the same percentage believe the programs should urge students not to have sexual intercourse. And, believe it or not, the sense of adults on this matter is actually confirmed by the young people who take the sex education courses. According to a recent survey, seventh and eighth graders say that the single greatest influence on their intention to engage or not to engage in intercourse is the fact that "It is against my values for me to have sex while I am a teenager." Social science researchers report that mere factual "knowledge alone has little impact, and that even peer pressure is less powerful" than what they call "the student's internalized beliefs and values."

How, then, might sex education do better in shaping the beliefs and values of our children? It could do better by underpinning the whole enterprise with a frank attention to the *real* issues, which has to do with responsibility for oneself and for one's actions. In the classroom, as at home, this means explaining and defending moral standards in the area of sex, and offering explicit moral guidance. For example, why not say in schools to students exactly what most American parents say at home: Children should not engage in sexual intercourse. Won't our children better understand such a message, and internalize it, if we say it to them—and if we say it in school as well as at home? Why isn't this message being taught in more classrooms? Why isn't this said?

In general, there seem to be three common excuses as to why the schools cannot teach such lessons in character.

First, it is said that, given the diversity of today's society, you could never determine whose values to put into the sex education curriculum, and anyway you should not indoctrinate the young with your beliefs or anyone else's. Apparently being "comfortable" with one's decision is the only consensual value left.

I cannot buy this reasoning because it seems to me that, when it comes to the well-being of our children, there are certain precepts to which virtually all Americans adhere. For example, I have never had a parent tell me that he or she would be offended by a teacher telling a class that it is better to postpone sex. Or that marriage is the best setting for sex, and in which to have and raise children. On the contrary, my impression is that the overwhelming majority of parents would gratefully welcome help in transmitting such values. And I don't think they would view this as indoctrination. It is simply ethical candor. To put students in the presence of a mature adult who speaks honestly and candidly to them in this way is not to violate their rights or to fail to respect their diversity.

Second, it is said by some that teenage sex is so pervasive now that we should simply face reality and surrender any quaint moral notions we continue to harbor about it. The kids are going to "do it" no matter what, so we ought to be trying to head off pregnancies by making sure they have contraceptives. As a member of one Washington lobbying organization said last month, "All of us wish teenagers wouldn't have sex, but Reagan and Bennett are dealing with the world as they would like it and we're looking at it as it is." Well, Reagan and Bennett *are* talking about the world as it is, and I would like to assert that it violates everything a school stands for simply to throw in the towel and say, "O.K. We give up. It's not right, but we can't seem to do anything about it, so we're not going to worry about it any more." That is no lesson in good character, either. Yes, sex entices from many parts of the culture. So does violence. So do drugs. But school is supposed to be better, and do better, and point to a better way. After all, we can accept reality while also trying to shape it and improve it. If school were no better than TV, parents would just leave their children to sit at home and watch the tube all day long. School is supposed to be better. Parents who are trying to do better for their children, who are trying to shape their children's character, need an ally in the schools. They do not need another opponent, or, almost as bad, an unprotesting "option" provider. And furthermore, not "everybody" is doing it, and we might wish to give those youngsters, half of our seventeen-year-olds, support and reinforcement, too.

There is simply no reason to assume that efforts to shape character in matters of sex are doomed to failure. In fact, there are encouraging signs to the contrary. A teen services program at Atlanta's Grady Memorial Hospital, for example, found that of the girls under age 16 it surveyed, nine out of ten wanted to learn how to say "no." Let me underline this. This is not just Reagan and Bennett talking, it's girls under 16 talking. Well, one way to help them say "no" is for adults who care to teach them the reasons to say "no," and to give them the necessary moral support and encouragement to keep on saying it.

The third excuse for giving up on the teaching of character in sex education was stated most recently by a panel of scientific experts. The much publicized report on teenage pregnancy by the National Research Council of the National Academy of Sciences draws one conclusion that few, I think, would disagree with: sexual activity among teenagers is intimately connected with issues of self-image. As the report states, "Several studies of social and psychological factors associated with adolescents' sexual behavior conclude that self-perception (not self-esteem)—that is, the sense of what and who one is, can be, and wants to be—is at the heart of teenagers' sexual decision making."

This would be a good starting point for any educational project aimed at helping our children understand ways in which premature sex hinders the possibilities of becoming who they can be, who they want to be. But, strangely enough, the National Research Council reverses course, saying, "[W]e currently know very little about how to effectively discourage unmarried teenagers from initiating intercourse." Rather than drawing a conclusion from the studies on self-perception, the council simply accepts the inevitability of teenage sexual activity, and urges "making contraceptive methods available and accessible to those who are sexually active and encouraging them to diligently use these methods" as "the surest strategy for pregnancy prevention."

I have a couple of observations about this. One, there is no evidence that making contraceptive methods more available is the surest strategy for preventing pregnancy, to say nothing about preventing sexual activity. Nor is it true that "we currently know very little about how to effectively discourage unmarried teenagers from initiating intercourse." It is true that what we know about such matters is not easily amenable to being measured and quantified. Nevertheless, we *do* know how to develop character and reinforce good values. We've known for quite a long time. As columnist William Raspberry has said, you do it the old-fashioned way. You make it clear to young people that there are moral considerations in life. You make it clear through habit, example, precept, and the inculcation of priorities. This is not only possible, it has been tested and proven through centuries of experience. It seems to me that the National Research Council is acting with an extravagantly single-minded blindness when it simply, in the name of science, ignores such experience, and offers instead a highly mechanical and bureaucratic solution: more widely available contraceptives in the schools.

The National Research Council's solution betrays a view of sex, and of life, that is dangerous for our children. For to suggest to our children that really the only things that matter about sexual activity are pleasure, or "comfort," or getting pregnant, or getting a sexually transmitted disease—to suggest that the act of sexual intimacy is not significant in other ways—is to offer them still another very bad lesson. Why? Because it's false. It's false because, as every adult knows, sex is inextricably connected to the psyche, to the soul, or if you don't like that term, to personality at its deepest levels. Rarely is it a mere riot of the glands that occurs and then is over and meaningless thereafter. Sexual intimacy changes things: it affects feelings, attitudes, one's self-image, one's view of another. Sexual activity never takes place outside the wider context of what is brought to it or left out of it by the persons who engage in it. It involves men and women in all their complexity; it involves their emotions, desires, and the often contradictory intentions that they bring with them, whether they mean to or not. It is, in other words, a quintessentially moral activity.

All societies have known this and have taken pains to regulate sexual activity. All societies have done so, sometimes wisely, sometimes not, because they have recognized that sex is fraught with mystery and passion, and that sex involves the person at the deepest level of being. As John Donne wrote, "Love's mysteries in *souls* do grow." Poets, novelists, philosophers, saints, and most psychiatrists have known that the power and beauty of sex lie precisely in the fact that it is *not* like anything else, that it is not just something you like to do or don't like to do. Far from being value-neutral, sex may be among the most value-loaded of any human activity. It does no good to try to sanitize or deny or ignore this truth. The act of sex involves deep springs of conduct. It is serious. It is complicated and has profound repercussions. And if we're going to deal with it in school, we'd better know this and acknowledge it. Otherwise, we should not let our schools have anything to do with it.

Our children, too, ought to know this. We ought to tell it to them. Not to tell them, to make sex out to be something less special and powerful than it is, is a dodge and a lie. It is just as much a dodge as denying the importance of sex or silencing a child who is awakening to an interest in sex. We serve children neither by denying their sexuality nor by making it a thing of no moral account.

With these thoughts in mind, I would like to offer a few principles that speak to the task of educating schoolchildren about sex, principles which I believe should inform curricular materials and textbooks, and by which such materials could be evaluated. These principles are, I believe, what most American parents are looking for in sex education.

First, we should recognize that sexual behavior is a matter of character and personality, and that we cannot be value neutral about it. Neutrality only confuses children, and may lead them to conclusions we wish them to avoid. Specifically: *sex education courses should teach children sexual restraint as a standard to uphold and follow.*

Second, in teaching restraint, courses should stress that *sex is not simply a physical or mechanical act.* We should explain to children that sex is tied to the deepest recesses of the personality. We should tell the truth; we should describe reality. We should explain that sex involves complicated feelings and emotions. Some of these are ennobling, and some of them, let us be truthful, can be cheapening of one's own finer impulses and cheapening to others.

Third, *sex education courses should speak up for the institution of the family.* To the extent possible, when they speak of sexual activity, courses should speak of it in the context of the institution of marriage. We should speak of the fidelity, commitment, and maturity of successful marriages as something for which our students should strive.

To the girls, teachers need to talk about readiness for mother-hood. And they must do more. They must not be afraid to use words like "modesty" and "chastity." Teachers and curriculum planners must be sure that sex education courses do not under-mine the values and beliefs that still lead most girls to see sexual modesty as a good thing. For it is a good thing, and a good word. Let us from time to time praise modesty. And teachers must not be afraid to teach lessons other girls have learned from bitter ex-perience. They should quote Lani Thompson, from T. C. Wil-liams High School in Alexandria, Virginia, who says of some of her friends: "I get upset when I see friends losing their virginity to some guy they've just met. Later, after the guy's dumped them, they come to me and say, 'I wish I hadn't done it.'"

And the boys need to hear these things too. In discussing these matters, teachers should not forget to talk to the boys. They should tell the boys what it is to be a father, what it is to be ready to be a father, what the responsibilities of being a father are. And they should tell them how the readiness and responsibility of be-ing a father should precede or at least accompany the acts which might make them fathers.

Fourth, *sex education courses should welcome parents and other adults as allies*. They should welcome parents into sex education classrooms as observers. If they do not, I would be suspicious. They should inform parents of the content of these courses, and they should encourage parents and children to talk to each other about sex. Studies show that when parents are the main source of sex education, children are less likely to engage in sex. This should come as no surprise when one remembers that the home is the crucible of character, and that parents are children's first and foremost teachers.

Many parents admit that they do not do enough to teach their children about sex. But still parents, more than anyone else, make the difference. Sex education courses can help remind those par-ents of their responsibilities. And these courses should encourage the individual counsel of priests, ministers, rabbis, and other adults who know a child well and who will take the time and offer the advice needed for the particular child. For it is the quality of the care and time that individuals take with other individuals which means the most in the formation of character.

Finally, schools, parents, and communities should pay atten-tion to who is teaching their children about sex. They should remember that teachers are role models for young people. And so *it is crucial that sex education teachers offer examples of good character* by the way they act, and by the ideals and convictions they must be willing to articulate to students. As Oxford's Mary Warnock has written, "you cannot teach morality without being committed to morality yourself; and you cannot be committed to morality yourself without holding that some things are right and others wrong."

These, then, are some of the principles I would like to see standing behind our schools' sex education courses. The truth, of course, is that what I think in this matter isn't as important as what you think. I don't have any schools. You've got the schools, and part of your job is to help inform the philosophies that guide them. Above all else, then, I would urge you, as you think about those philosophies, to make sure your schools are teaching our children the truth. Sometimes the simplest way to recognize the truth is to consult common sense. Let me urge you to follow your common sense. Don't be intimidated by the sexologists, by the so-called sex-ed experts, by the sex technicians. Character education is mostly a matter of common sense. If sex education courses are prepared to deal with the truth, with reality in all its complexity, with the hard truths of the human condition, then they should be welcome in our schools. But if sex education courses are not prepared to tell the truth, if instead they want to simplify or distort or omit certain aspects of these realities in this very important realm of human life, then we should let them go out of business. If sex education courses do not help in the effort to provide an education in character, then let them be gone from the presence of our children.

IN SEARCH OF PEACE

THIS HONOR BELONGS TO ALL THE SURVIVORS[1]
ELIE WIESEL[2]

Ever since he emerged from a Nazi death camp in April 1945, Elie Wiesel, who lost his parents and a sister in the Holocaust, has dedicated his life to telling the story of the German World War II concentration camps. It was Wiesel who first used the word "holocaust" to describe the treatment of the victims. Known as the "conscience of the Holocaust," Wiesel has worked to ensure that mankind never forgets the horrors of that dark episode in human history. Congressman Tom Lantos said of Wiesel,

> More than any other he has helped us to understand—to the extent that understanding is possible—the significance of that nightmare. His voice has been the clearest in calling for us to create conditions to prevent the repetition of that outrage. His thoughtful and moving words have significance for all of us. (*Congressional Record*, May 3, 1984, p. E1948)

On December 10, 1986, the Norwegian Nobel Committee honored Wiesel for his efforts to prevent a recurrence of the Holocaust by presenting to him the Nobel Peace Prize. The distinguished award is something of an anomaly because the money used to establish the prizes came from a financial empire based on the invention of dynamite and other explosives by Alfred Nobel, who, in the words of Tony Gray,

> . . . in his day probably did more than any other single human being to make possible the horrors of prenuclear war. Indeed, Nobel's inventions comprised the basic ingredients of the holocaust of the two world wars and they remain a stock-in-trade of terrorists everywhere. (*Champions of Peace*, Birmingham, England, 1962, p. 12)

The prize was presented to Wiesel by Egil Aarvik, chairman of the Norwegian Nobel Committee. In his speech, Aarvik pointed out that the first Nobel peace award presented 50 years earlier went to Carol von Ossietskey, a German pacifist who did not survive the Hitler regime, and that the present award was honoring one who did. Aarvik recalled Wiesel's comment on the birth of his son that at first he felt sorry for anyone being born into such a world as ours, but that he almost immediately began to see his son as a bridge between the past and the future. For that reason, he asked the 14-year-old boy, Shlomo Elisha, to stand and receive the

[1] © The Nobel Foundation. The speech was delivered in the Aula Festival Hall at the University of Oslo in Oslo, Norway, shortly before 1 P.M. (7 A.M. Eastern Standard Time), on December 10, 1986.

[2] For biographical note, see Appendix.

medal along with his father.

The ceremony took place in the Aula Festival Hall at the University of Oslo in Norway. Preceding Wiesel's brief acceptance speech, an orchestra played an Edvard Grieg nocturne. Steve Fagin described the scene:

> Wiesel strode into the vast hall shortly before 1 P.M. (7 A.M. Eastern Standard Time) to thunderous applause from an audience of more than 800 diplomats, friends, relatives, and fellow concentration camp survivors. After greeting Norwegian King Olav V, he approached the gilt-trimmed lectern, put on a skull cap, and said a prayer of thanks. Then, after calling his teenage son Shlomo to his side, he took several moments to compose himself before beginning his speech. (New London, Connecticut, *Day*, December 10, 1986)

New York Times reporter Francis X. Clines described Wiesel's acceptance speech:

> Elie Wiesel dared not speak for the dead today as he accepted the Nobel Peace Prize. "No one may interpret their mutilated dreams and visions. . . . " Instead, the weary-faced author and teacher, 58 years old, fought back tears and eventually smiled and spoke for the living in accepting the prize "as one who has emerged from that kingdom of night." . . . Except for the discordant sound of camera shutters whirring, . . . his audience was absolutely silent. (*New York Times*, December 11, 1986, p. 1)

The entire ceremony lasted one hour. Many in attendance wept openly, and Wiesel paused often to regain control of his emotions. As Wiesel stepped down from the dais at the end of his acceptance speech, "a sea of people surged toward" him. "Norwegians out on the street applauded, too, as he walked from the hall into the dark afternoon and was seen smiling, hugging his family and friends." (*New York Times*, December 11, 1986, p. 1)

Elie Wiesel's speech: It is with a profound sense of humility that I accept the honor you have chosen to bestow upon me. I know: Your choice transcends me. This both frightens and pleases me.

It frightens me because I wonder: Do I have the right to represent the multitudes who have perished? Do I have the right to accept this great honor on their behalf? I do not. That would be presumptuous. No one may speak for the dead, no one may interpret their mutilated dreams and visions.

It pleases me because I may say that this honor belongs to all the survivors and their children, and through us, to the Jewish people with whose destiny I have always identified.

I remember: It happened yesterday or eternities ago. A young Jewish boy discovered the kingdom of night. I remember his bewilderment, I remember his anguish. It all happened so fast. The ghetto. The deportation. The sealed cattle car. The fiery altar upon which the history of our people and the future of mankind were meant to be sacrificed.

I remember: He asked his father: "Can this be true? This is the 20th century, not the Middle Ages. Who would allow such crimes to be committed? How could the world remain silent?"

And now the boy is turning to me: "Tell me," he asks. "What have you done with my future? What have you done with your life?"

And I tell him that I have tried. That I have tried to keep memory alive, that I have tried to fight those who would forget. Because if we forget, we are guilty, we are accomplices.

And then I explained to him how naive we were, that the world did know and remain silent. And that is why I swore never to be silent whenever and wherever human beings endure suffering and humiliation. We must always take sides. Neutrality helps the oppressor, never the victim. Silence encourages the tormentor, never the tormented.

Sometimes we must interfere. When human lives are endangered, when human dignity is in jeopardy, national borders and sensitivities become irrelevant. Wherever men or women are persecuted because of their race, religion or political views, that place must—at that moment—become the center of the universe.

Of course, since I am a Jew profoundly rooted in my people's memory and tradition, my first response is to Jewish fear, Jewish needs, Jewish crises. For I belong to a traumatized generation, one that experienced the abandonment and solitude of our people. It would be unnatural for me not to make Jewish priorities my own: Israel, Soviet Jewry, Jews in Arab lands.

But there are others as important to me. Apartheid is, in my view, as abhorrent as anti-Semitism. To me, Andrei Sakharov's isolation is as much of a disgrace as Iosif Begun's imprisonment. As is the denial of Solidarity and its leader Lech Walesa's right to dissent. And Nelson Mandela's interminable imprisonment.

There is so much injustice and suffering crying out for our attention: Victims of hunger, or racism and political persecution, writers and poets, prisoners in so many lands governed by the left and by the right. Human rights are being violated on every continent. More people are oppressed than free.

And then, too, there are the Palestinians to whose plight I am sensitive but whose methods I deplore. Violence and terrorism are not the answer. Something must be done about their suffering, and soon. I trust Israel, for I have faith in the Jewish people. Let Israel be given a chance, let hatred and danger be removed from her horizons, and there will be peace in and around the Holy Land.

Yes, I have faith. Faith in God and even in His creation. Without it no action would be possible. And action is the only remedy to indifference: the most insidious danger of all. Isn't this the meaning of Alfred Nobel's legacy? Wasn't his fear of war a shield against war?

There is much to be done, there is much that can be done. One person—a Raoul Wallenberg, an Albert Schweitzer, one person of integrity, can make a difference, a difference of life and death. As long as one dissident is in prison, our freedom will not be true. As long as one child is hungry, our lives will be filled with anguish and shame.

What all these victims need above all is to know that they are not alone; that we are not forgetting them, that when their voices are stifled we shall lend them ours, that while their freedom depends on ours, the quality of our freedom depends on theirs.

This is what I say to the young Jewish boy wondering what I have done with his years. It is in his name that I speak to you and that I express to you my deepest gratitude. No one is as capable of gratitude as one who has emerged from the kingdom of night.

We know that every moment is a moment of grace, every hour an offering; not to share them would mean to betray them. Our lives no longer belong to us alone; they belong to all those who need us desperately.

Thank you Chairman Aarvik. Thank you, members of the Nobel Committee. Thank you, people of Norway, for declaring on this singular occasion that our survival has meaning for mankind.

THE PLACE OF RELIGIOUS VALUES
IN FOREIGN POLICY

TERRORISM[1]
F. FORRESTER CHURCH[2]

On the night of April 14, 1986, the United States launched a series of air strikes by 18 air force bombers flown from England and additional bombers from naval aircraft carriers in the Mediterranean on five targets in Libya. The raids were directed at what the White House called "terrorist centers" and military bases.

The purpose of the strikes was to punish Libyan leader Colonel Muammar Khadafi, whom President Ronald Reagan had called the "mad dog of the Middle East." In a nationally televised speech following the raids, the president said that the United States had "solid evidence" that Libya was behind an explosion that killed an American sergeant in a West Berlin discotheque frequented by U.S. troops.

The 11 minutes of bombing resulted in the death of 37 people and the injury of 93 others, as well as the destruction of residential buildings and the French embassy. While the administration insisted that Colonel Khadafi had not been a target, U.S. planes dropped four 2,000-pound bombs on the barracks where he lived. Although Khadafi was not harmed, the attack killed his 15-month-old daughter and wounded two of his sons.

Response to the raid differed greatly. According to a *New York Times*/CBS News poll, the American people overwhelmingly supported the bombing, despite widespread fears that it would lead to more international terrorism. The survey revealed that 77 percent of the public approved and only 14 percent disapproved. (Adam Clymer, *New York Times*, April 17, 1986, p. A23) World reaction to the U.S. attack, however, was voluble and almost entirely hostile. Of the members of the North Atlantic Treaty Organization [NATO], only Canada and Britain supported the American strike. In Britain, a poll by *The Times* of London showed that only 29 percent of the public approved the bombing.

While the majority of Americans approved of the raid on Libya, some were deeply disturbed by the attack. One objector was the Reverend Dr. F. Forrester Church, pastor of the All Souls Unitarian Church in New York City. In his sermon on Sunday, April 20, 1986, Reverend Church told the congregation that he had waited all week for someone to say what he "felt so very deeply," but that with few exceptions, no one was speaking out against the bombings that in his conviction were "terribly, terribly wrong." In a note to the editor of this volume, Church explained, "I discarded the sermon I had prepared for this Sunday, changing my topic in

[1]Delivered to the congregation of All Souls Unitarian Church in New York City at 11:30 A.M. on April 20, 1986.

[2]For biographical note, see Appendix.

order to respond to the issue that was foremost on all of our minds right then."

Dr. Church delivered his sermon to an audience of approximately 550 members and friends of the All Souls Unitarian Church on the corner of 80th Street and Lexington Avenue in Manhattan at 11:30 A.M.

F. Forrester Church's speech: In some ways this is going to be a very difficult sermon for me to deliver. For one thing, I feel so strongly about what I am going to say, that I am sure to lose my balance here or there. Passion is not a bad thing, but rarely does it contribute to objectivity. Also, I feel most comfortable with my own views, when I can pose to myself and for others an almost but not quite convincing argument against them. As I have said to you before, much of the time I end up fashioning 100% decisions on 60% convictions. Though this is uncomfortable at times, it does have its advantages. One advantage is that almost never am I tempted to despise those who think differently than I do. After all, I myself could very well be one of them.

But today, I am absolutely sure that I am right. And that worries me. It worries me for two reasons. One is that I am not accustomed to feeling this way. And the other is that judging from the public opinion polls, almost no one in this country agrees with me.

Think about it. Never in the recent history of our country has there been so strong a consensus as there apparently is today around the President's decision to bomb Libya in reprisal for the Libyan directed bombing of a West German nightclub, in which one American G.I. was killed. According to the *New York Times*, 77% of Americans favor this decision while just 14% oppose it, even though a majority of those questioned also believe that this action will increase terrorist activity, not diminish it. At the same time, the President's favorable rating on his conducting of our foreign policy has soared this week to an unprecedented 76%. As of yesterday, not one Democratic U.S. Senator had raised his voice in opposition to the bombing. The only questions that have been raised were by Senators Hatfield, Weicker, and Mathias, all members of the President's own party. In the House of Representatives, according to Ann Lewis, the executive director of Americans for Democratic Action—who spoke at an American Friends Service Committee seminar on negotiation this Friday which I was moderating—only a handful of Congressmen have dared, or seen fit, to raise their voices in opposition: Edwards and Dellums of California; Conyers of Michigan; and Schroeder of Colorado.

All week, in fact, I waited for someone to say what I felt so very deeply, and with the exception of Alexander Cockburn in the *Wall Street Journal* and Tom Wicker in the *New York Times*, almost no one did. On the CNN Crossfire program where Tom Braden and Robert Novak debate guests who take opposite positions on issues, not a single member of Congress apparently could be found who would speak out against the bombing, and so the opposition view was offered by a British member of Parliament who just happened to be in Washington.

And yet, throughout the week my conviction grew that this action was terribly, terribly wrong. This morning I want to tell you why.

Let me begin with something I said last week in my sermon on "Paranoia and Power."

Jesus taught us that we must not answer evil with evil. And history teaches that we must choose our enemies carefully because we will become like them. Not only that, but when we do, unconscious of the good in our enemies and terrified by their evil, we eventually will become like them at their least attractive. Accordingly, when we react to terrorism with bombs of our own, killing innocent civilians and even children, we too become terrorists.

This past week, we have added a tragic new chapter to the primitive ethics of an eye for an eye and a tooth for a tooth. It could be subtitled "a baby for a baby." One infant is blown out of the side of an airplane, another blown out of her crib by our bombs.

Former President Jimmy Carter said in an interview on Thursday, that if his daughter, Amy, had been killed in this manner, he would devote his life to exacting revenge upon whoever had done it. This is not a part of Christian theology, but it is certainly understandable from a human point of view. On the other hand, such revenge is a part of the teachings of Islam. Friday, in the streets of Tripoli, angry citizens and religious leaders were calling for a Holy War to be declared against the United States all around the world. Our government claims that we have taken a major step to end terrorism by showing that no terrorist act will go unanswered. This betrays a complete lack of understanding both of the nature of terrorism itself, and of the Islamic faith. What we forget is this. If, as they are often taught, instant bliss is the reward for death in a holy cause, religious zealots—

whether terrorist, holy innocent, or both—are delighted to don the martyr's crown. And even if they don't win a free ride to heaven, here on earth their self-proclaimed holy cause will surely be advanced. Tertullian, an early church father, said to Christian martyrs that "the blood of the martyrs is the seed of the church." By creating new martyrs in the nation of Islam, we too seed the dark clouds of terrorism all around the globe.

This, then, is my first major concern. But acting according to fear, frustration, and anger, we have not reduced but rather added to the level of violence in the world. Not only that, but we have become a full partner in that violence. We have also added to the level of terror in the hearts of our European allies.

This is not to say that the President's action, and the American people's response, is not powered by deep moral outrage. Of course it is. We are morally motivated people. We speak a public language that is filled with religious and moral metaphor. We paint our enemies as demonic, and often their actions justify such a title. We also speak of evil empires, and thus create a mythos for Armageddon that pits the powers of good against the powers of evil.

Certainly, there is no question in any of our minds that terrorism is demonic. The question is, how do you fight the devil? We have chosen to fight him with his own instruments. And we have chosen as our pretext self-defense. Sometimes, we have no choice, as in World War II in our struggle against Hitler. Then, we answered our allies' call to protect them against German imperialism and the evils of fascism.

Today, however, our allies, whether rightly or wrongly, are as wary of us as they are of our common enemy. Somehow, we have lost the moral initiative. Because the enemy, in this case Colonel Khadafi, is so pernicious, we have a hard time perceiving that anything we might do to punish him could be anything but right, regardless of the consequences. But here, the consequences as well as the means of accomplishing them are patently counterproductive. All we have done is further isolate ourselves. In the eyes of our allies, we again have become part of the problem, rather than part of the solution.

I don't know what the answer to terrorism is. And it is frustrating not to have a quick-fix, a solution that will surely work. Because of this frustration, to counter our sense of helplessness we are tempted to try anything. I understand that. But when our solution adds to the problem, even from a pragmatic point of view, without any consideration of the moral issues involved, we surely should forbear. One thing we learned in Vietnam was that we could not successfully wage a conventional war against guerrillas in the jungle. Soon we shall learn that we cannot wage a conventional war against tiny bands of violent zealots either. There is one thing we can do, however, if we had the strength and patience and confidence to do so. We could hold to the moral high ground. We could remember what we were taught as little children, that two wrongs do not make a right, and that good ends do not justify evil means. We could model a different code than that modeled by those we despise.

Would it work? I think, in some ways, that it has worked in the case of Yassar Arafat. Through his actions, he has finally convicted himself in the court of world opinion. He and the PLO are no longer celebrated in the Arab world, but rather seen as liabilities.

Also, in the case of Khadafi, save for the pretext that we now have given him to muster the support of his Arab neighbors, over the years he too has become an embarrassment to them. Lacking a common enemy, which we have provided him with a vengeance, it is likely that the weakness of his country's economy and the growing opposition to his flamboyant and idiosyncratic leadership within Libya itself, would bring him down.

And who knows, this still may happen. But, even if it does, I deeply believe that our bombing of Libya was wrong. Whether or not the perception is a fair one, in fighting terrorism in Rambo or Lone Ranger fashion, in moving outside the courts of law and the courts of world opinion, we have confused the moral issue, the question of good and evil. This does three things. It compromises us. It alienates our friends. And it has an incendiary effect upon the very zealots we are trying to subdue.

This past week has been more riddled with terrorist incidents and terrifying close calls than any in memory. And who is being blamed? Not the perpetrators themselves. No, we are being blamed. The demonstrations in the streets of England and France and Germany are not against Colonel Khadafi. They are against us.

I have been thinking a great deal this week about my father, Frank Church, who served in the U.S. Senate for 24 years. I miss him intensely right now. I miss his voice. So let me close, not with my own words, but with his.

In 1975 the Senate Intelligence Committee, which he chaired, uncovered evidence of five unsuccessful CIA-sponsored assassination plots against foreign leaders. In issuing his report my father wrote, "The United States must not adopt the tactics of the enemy. Means are as important as ends. Crisis makes it tempting to ignore the wise restraint that makes us free; but each time we do so, each time the means we use are wrong, our inner strength, the strength which makes us free, is lessened."

Elsewhere he said, speaking of the founders of our country, "They acted on their faith, not their fear. They did not believe in fighting fire with fire; crime with crime; evil with evil; or delinquency by becoming delinquents." Amen.

WHAT IS TRUTH?[1]
PAUL MOORE, JR.[2]

An article published on November 3, 1986, in *Al Shiraa,* a Syrian magazine in Lebanon, revealed that the United States government had for some time been engaged in secret negotiations with Iran to supply the Iranians with arms in return for the release of hostages. The revelation made front page headlines throughout the country. Ten days after the appearance of the article, President Reagan admitted to a "secret diplomatic mission to Iran," but insisted there was no weapons-for-hostages swap. On November 25, Attorney General Edwin Meese III revealed that profits from the Iranian arms sales had been diverted to the "Contra" rebels in Nicaragua, apparently in contravention of United States law. Of the principals accused of involvement in the plan, Lieutenant Colonel Oliver L. North was fired and Rear Admiral John M. Poindexter resigned. Following the appointment by President Reagan of a three-member commission to "get to the bottom" of the growing scandal, both North and Poindexter invoked the fifth amendment when called to testify before the Senate Select Committee on Intelligence.

The events were among other developments disturbing many Americans as 1986 drew to a close. The concerned included clergymen. In an article appearing in the *New York Times* on December 25, 1986, Dennis Hevesi reported:

> Crises in confidence in government and race relations were on the minds of several of the city's spiritual leaders yesterday as they prepared what they would say today when their parishioners gathered

[1]Delivered to the congregation at the Cathedral of St. John the Divine in New York City at 11:00 P.M. on December 24, 1986.
[2]For biographical note, see Appendix.

to celebrate Christmas. . . .

The Episcopal Bishop of New York, Paul Moore Jr., was not without hope in the sermon he prepared for delivery at the Cathedral of St. John the Divine. If anything, he said, he wanted to call forth the light of truth in speaking of "a darkness on our land, a cloud of darkness over our leaders."

"The image of our nation's greatness no longer shines clear and strong across the world," he said.

Still, the Bishop wrote, "The prince of peace is also the prince of truth. Let the religious community, therefore, step forward during this holy season with a demand for truth from our government. We call upon leaders and lay people alike to recognize in the White House crisis a threat to the spiritual integrity of the nation. The religious community must demand an end to these months of cover-up and evasion. For it is the truth that sets us free."

Bishop Moore delivered his sermon to approximately 5,000 people at the Cathedral of St. John the Divine in New York City at 11:00 P.M. on Christmas eve, December 24, 1986.

Paul Moore, Jr.'s speech:

The people who walked in the darkness have seen a great light; those who dwell in a land of deep darkness, on them has light shined. Thou hast multiplied the nation, Thou hast increased its joy. They rejoice before Thee as with joy at the harvest. . . . For the yoke of his burden and the staff of his shoulder, the rod of his oppressor Thou hast broken. (Isaiah 9:2) In those days a decree went out from Caesar Augustus that all the world should be taxed. (Luke 2:1)

Today there is a darkness on our land, a cloud of darkness over our leaders, and the image of our great nation no longer shines clear and strong across the world because we have abandoned truth. But there is hope; there is even certainty that truth will return. For the light of Christ shines strong. "The people who walked in darkness have seen a great light; those who dwell in a land of deep darkness, on them has light shined."

The world has not changed much over the last two thousand years. The reason Jesus was born in Bethlehem, far from home, the reason Jesus was born to a homeless couple, was because they had to travel to the city of Joseph's ancestors, Bethlehem, in order to be taxed by the Roman Empire. Caesar Augustus had declared that all the world would be taxed to support the defense of the Roman Empire, the so-called *Pax Romana.* The *Pax Romana* was the imposing of the power and will of Rome upon all the peoples within the far-flung borders of the empire. All the tribes, ethnic groups, small nations, all were kept down under the heel of Rome. And the vulgar Roman culture, the pompous architecture of the empire, was dumped across the world. We still see ruins of it incongruously placed within other more delicate local cultures. Caesar Augustus imposed the rule of Rome and the exploitive economics of Rome upon Medes, Parthians, Egyptians, Syrians, Jews, and other peoples as well. It is indeed ironic that he who was to be hailed the prince of peace was born at Bethlehem because of the needs of the military complex of Empire.

Politics dogged the life of Jesus from start to finish. The wise men came from afar to seek the prince of peace. Naturally, they first went to Jerusalem where their arrival struck terror into Herod's heart. He asked them to go find this king, this young prince who had just been born into the world, and to report the location of his birth. Herod was the puppet of Rome and had sold his soul to the execution of its policy of domination. He feared that a native-born king of the Jews would rise up against him and that a powerful mix of religion and nationalism would overthrow him. And so, with the violence of threatened absolute power, he ordered the slaughter of all the children of the region lest Rome's rule and his own be challenged.

The political situation is only slightly different today. There are *two* Empires, not one, ranging across the world, taxing people to support their military/industrial complexes, which in turn become the means of suppressing peoples who seek self-determination, peoples who seek freedom. Innocents are still slaughtered: the innocents of Afghanistan, of Nicaragua, of El Salvador. And as the vortex of world power swirls around the Middle East, Bethlehem itself is once more at the center; Bethlehem is on the West Bank.

All this is obvious; but you know, Herod was right. The child was dangerous. Thirty years later, the child of Bethlehem was to stand before Pontius Pilate and be asked the question, "What is truth?". At that time it was not any longer simply a puppet king who was threatened, but also the religious establishment which had cast its lot with the state. And Pilate even felt that Rome itself, in some strange way, was challenged by the message of the young religious radical. And so it was. Their conversation went like this:

Pilate: Are you the king of the Jews?
Jesus: Do you say this of your own accord; or did others say it to you about me?
Pilate: Am I a Jew? Your own nation and the chief priests have handed you over to me. What have you done?

Jesus: My kingship is not of this world. If my kingship were of this world, my servants would fight that I might not be handed over to the Jews. But my kingship is not of this world.
Pilate: So you are a king?
Jesus: You say that I am a king. For this I was born; for this I have come into the world: to bear witness to the truth. Everyone who is of the truth hears my voice.
Pilate: What is truth?

Does that sound familiar? And two thousand years later, the child of Bethlehem is still bearing witness to the truth, is still challenging the rule of oppressive empires.

At Christmas we associate Christ with love and peace. We speak of the prince of peace and good will toward men. But the word of God is also the word of truth. Without truth, law has no foundation; without law, justice has no foundation; without justice, freedom has no foundation. And yet nothing puts more fear into the heart of corrupt rulers than the threat of truth.

The sickness of the soul of a nation is measured not only by the loss of compassion for her own people, not only by the tyranny which seeks to rule the world by arms; the sickness of a nation's soul is most clearly manifested in its arrogant disregard of truth. For when truth is jettisoned, the fabric of society is torn, righteousness disintegrates, the center does not hold. In such a case the left and right, all the special interests and ideologies, create a free-for-all of power—and [it is] the people who are trampled on.

Truth can die in an Orwellian slump of doublespeak and confusion. Each time the White House loses integrity by an action contrary to truth, the nation dies by that much, and the people's sensitivity to truth becomes blinded by that much. But do not despair; Christ came as a light to shine in our darkness, to lead us on a path toward truth. Christmas is a time for those who rejoice in the coming of love to pray as well for the coming of truth into our own lives and the life of our nation. "I have come into the world to bear witness to the truth." This is our mandate, too, as members of His body.

The shining word of God cannot co-exist with the foul darkness of lies and the stale fumes of corruption. The shining love of God cannot co-exist with a nation or nations which, for dubious economic and political aims, are willing to slaughter thousands upon thousands of innocents. The shining word of compassion cannot co-exist with a government that leaves the poor of its own land starving and homeless in order to raise funds for weapons to kill the poor of other lands. But before dealing with these weaknesses of our leadership, we must have truth.

Look at the disaster in the White House. Two high ranking military officers, whose comrades-in-arms over the years have risked—even given their lives—to defend our country, dare not even risk their reputations to defend the integrity of our foreign policy. High ranking executives seem to lie to avoid the political consequences of the truth.

Congress shares the blame, for Congress was too timid to block our murderous Central American policy, to stand up and say no to a policy built on lies from the very beginning. This winking at untruth by Congress has allowed total blindness to truth to envelope the executive branch.

Why are people not more aroused? Are we becoming so used to lies that truth no longer matters? We have lost compassion. The homeless and starving walk our streets, in every city of the nation, and we no longer even see them. We have grown used to civic cruelty. Are we also to lose trust, integrity, and truth? Do we now have to ask, as Pilate asked two thousand years ago, "What is truth?", because we do not know?

The prince of peace is also the prince of truth. Let the religious community, therefore, step forward during this holy season with a demand for truth from our government. We call upon leaders and lay people alike to recognize in the White House crisis a threat to the spiritual integrity of the nation. We have been through this before. The religious community must demand an end to these months of cover-up and evasion. For it is the truth that sets us free.

Come my friends, rise up! Your king and saviour draweth nigh. Be witnesses to Him who said "I have come into the world to bear witness to the truth." This is the great message of Christmas, the harsh and wonderful judgment of truth for which we, as members of Christ's body, are responsible.

In the same way that Herod and Pilate shook in the presence of truth, in the same way governments shake in truth's light, so do we as individuals. And, as the prince of truth is born today in our lives, so do we as individuals need to examine our own integrity, our own sense of truth, so that we at least can be instruments of truth in the world.

We shudder at the presence of the prince of truth, but we also shudder at the presence of the prince of love. Yes, we come to the manger to be ministered to by Him, but there are homes into which Christmas brings pain and even torture.

Therefore, as I look forth upon you, my friends, tonight and know something of the agony which may be present in many a soul coming to this holy place, I ask you as I have asked you over the years, to open that hurt—that agony—to the touch of the love of Jesus; to open up whatever lie is corrupting your own life, to the surgery of the prince of truth; to trust, to trust, to trust in His love and to have the courage to trust in His truth, so that the pure presence of His love may find in you a home for the infant Christ.

SHAPING THE FUTURE

TWO CHALLENGES:
SOUTH AFRICA AND URBAN EDUCATION[1]
John E. Jacob[2]

The National Urban League held its annual conference in San Francisco for four days in mid-July, 1986. From the beginning of the year, leaders of the civil rights organization had been increasingly outspoken in their disappointment with the Reagan administration's policies towards blacks. As early as January, in its annual "State of Black America" report, the organization noted that the economic gap between blacks and whites had widened in 1985 and was wider then than at any time since 1970. League President John E. Jacob noted, "The state of black America today is deeply troubled." (David T. Cook, *Christian Science Monitor*, January 24, 1986, p. 1)

Although the league's tax exempt status prohibits it from direct lobbying on issues, the comments of Jacob and other speakers at the San Francisco conference were indicative of the more activist role the league had begun to play. Jacob's keynote address was described as "one of his strongest attacks ever on the Reagan Administration, its civil rights policies, and its policy of 'constructive engagement' toward South Africa." (Lena Williams, *New York Times*, July 21, 1986, p. A18) Other speakers at the conference who reflected Jacob's disillusionment with the Reagan administration included Benjamin L. Hooks, executive director of the National Association for the Advancement of Colored People, and Clifton R. Wharton, Jr., chancellor of the State University of New York.

Two days after the convention of the National Urban League, John Jacob delivered an address to the Commonwealth Club of San Francisco. The invitation afforded Jacob an opportunity to take his message to a group of business executives who might be able to exert influence in support of his aims. Acknowledging the achievements of the club, Jacob said, "It is a great honor to join you in this distinguished forum. The Commonwealth Club has long contributed to informed debate of issues of importance to our society." In his address, he focused on two issues related to the business community: American investment in South Africa and urban education.

The 50-year-old Jacob had worked with the National Urban League for more than 21 years. He had taken over leadership of the organization from Vernon E. Jordan, Jr., in 1981. In recent years, according to some observers, Jacob "has become more comfortable with public discussion of issues that were not in the past talked about." (*New York Times*, July 7, 1986, p. 6)

---

[1]Delivered to the Commonwealth Club of California in San Francisco at a noon luncheon in a banquet room of the Sheraton Palace Hotel on July 25, 1986.
[2]For biographical note, see Appendix.

Jacob delivered his speech at a noon luncheon meeting of the Commonwealth Club in a ballroom of the Sheraton Palace Hotel in San Francisco on July 25, 1986. His audience consisted of approximately 130 members of the organization. Founded in 1903, the educational club's 16,000 members include business executives, lawyers, educators, and students.

John E. Jacob's speech: It is a great honor to join you in this distinguished forum. The Commonwealth Club has long contributed to informed public debate of issues of importance to our society. The National Urban League provides a similar forum. Earlier this week, we held our 76th annual conference here in San Francisco, where invited speakers and participants represented a broad variety of views. There were Democrats, Republicans, congressmen, cabinet secretaries, business and labor leaders, academics, representatives of community groups, and others, all taking part in the nation's largest forum on race relations.

Two important issues discussed at our Conference impact strongly on the business community, and I would like to discuss them with you today. One is South Africa. The other is the challenge of urban education.

The issue of South Africa has been a troubling one for American business, especially for multinational corporations with investments in that country. Traditionally, business holds that companies must obey the laws of the states in which they operate and refrain from political activities. But because of the unique nature of South African society, that traditional stance has had to be modified.

Corporations feel the need to justify their presence in South Africa. They claim that their enlightened policies and their adherence to the Sullivan Code undermine the foundations of apartheid and offer alternative routes of development. And many point to their continuing responsibilities to the black employees who would suffer if they left. More recently, many U.S.-based corporations have been outspoken in their opposition to apartheid. They have publicly pressured the government there to change its policies.

But the situation in South Africa has changed for the worse. Hopes that the Botha regime would be amenable to change have been dashed. It refuses to consider any form of real power-sharing, raids neighboring countries, and imposes a state of emergency that effectively destroys its claim to be part of the community of civilized states.

The justifications for a continued American business presence in South Africa were based on the inevitability of change in the system, of enlarged freedoms for the black majority, and of the likelihood of an eventual negotiated settlement between white and black South Africans. Those prospects have been trampled into the dust by an intransigent government and by the dynamics of an awakened black majority unwilling to defer freedom to some distant time when the white minority becomes more enlightened.

South Africa is unique in the world today. And because it is unique, it demands a unique response. Nowhere else does a minority oppress a majority solely on racial grounds. Nowhere else are the majority of people denied citizenship on racial grounds. Nowhere else is a majority excluded from political participation solely on racial grounds. And nowhere else do we confront the terrible prospect of racial warfare.

Given that unique situation, the administration's policy of constructive engagement was doomed to failure. It was flawed from the start, for it was limited to engagement with the government of South Africa, and not with representatives of the black majority. The administration continues to think it can nudge South Africa into making reforms.

But after five years of constructive engagement, Nelson Mandela remains in prison, the government jails black and white leaders, and it refuses to negotiate. And the time when "reforms" could satisfy black aspirations is long gone. The real issue is and always was political power—and that requires negotiations between the minority government and black leadership to work out new constitutional arrangements.

The United States can best help that process by substituting a policy of constructive pressure for the failed policy of constructive engagement.

One form of constructive pressure is sanctions. Sanctions are often said to be unworkable, but if they are so feeble, why did we impose sanctions on Poland, on Nicaragua, on Libya? And why does South Africa expend so much energy trying to convince us not to impose them? In fact, sanctions are an effective way to bring economic pressures, to register moral indignation, and to demonstrate support for the black majority in South Africa.

It is in America's interest to be on the side of South Africa's future, not its past. And the way to do that is not through public relations gimmicks, but by changing our policy. Without a drastic shift in U.S. policy a future black government of South Africa may adopt policies that could destroy our interests there.

The Administration's policy—or lack of it—forces U.S. companies to choose between voluntarily withdrawing from that country now or being expelled from it later. They have been victimized by what is, in effect, the privatization of U.S. foreign policy. They have had to do what the State Department should have been doing: fighting apartheid. Their pressures on Pretoria have been welcome, but they went to the wrong address. Washington needs to become the focus of corporate pressure.

For it is in Washington that U.S. policies must be framed and implemented. And it is Washington's failure to identify America with the black struggle for freedom that left U.S. companies dangling in the wind.

Corporate America must insist that the Administration take a tough line with South Africa, that Washington should make foreign policy and not abandon its responsibilities to corporations that have neither the right nor the inclination to do so. The corporate reasons for continuing to do business in South Africa have eroded. It would be best for American companies still there to leave now, as many have already done. By leaving now—as a powerful demonstration of opposition to apartheid—American multinationals can eventually return to a new, free South Africa. Voluntary withdrawal is not a measure to be taken lightly. But it would send a powerful message to black and white South Africans, a message that says corporate America cannot conduct business in a social atmosphere of terror and oppression and in an economic atmosphere of uncertainty and turmoil.

Many companies today are actively considering withdrawal. I urge them to withdraw from South Africa, the sooner the better.

I recognize the difficulty of such a decision and make no moral judgment of those who believe even now that they must remain. But there is a moral judgment to be made about governmental actions. And there can be no moral justification for the United States government to continue policies that treat apartheid as a nuisance rather than as an inhuman evil.

Time is no longer running out on South Africa: it has run out. And time is no longer running out on American policies toward South Africa: it has run out. Washington and our allies should implement a new policy of constructive pressure on South Africa, including sanctions, friendly ties with the anti-apartheid forces, and aggressive support for the black South African majority.

A second major issue at our conference was education.

The black economy is a disaster area, as jobs held by black workers have been wiped out through massive imports and by the restructuring that is transforming our economy.

I visited East Asia last fall, and saw some of the competition. There is no way we can compete against workers making pennies an hour. And there is no way we can maintain our standard of living by trying to compete on labor costs.

As employers seek higher productivity through automation, jobs are lost. Some are also created, but those new jobs demand higher skills. And that means we need a vastly improved education system. The black economic fate is directly tied to our ability to function in a restructured national economy. It is imperative that our children's schools equip them with the technical and analytical skills employers seek.

On the basis of past experience, that might not be considered good news. In the past, blacks were told to get educated and then when we turned up with college degrees we were told: "we don't hire blacks." Ours is bitter history of black scientists working as porters and black lawyers working in the post office.

But that's the past. The future has to be different. In part, because the hiring of blacks has become institutionalized to the point where it's irreversible, no matter what the Administration says about affirmative action. In that regard, the Supreme Court's decisions earlier this month amount to a bright green signal for constructive affirmative action plans.

Minority hiring is also irreversible because of demographic realities. The workforce is one-fourth nonwhite. Minorities are an increasing share of the population: for the first time there aren't enough white males to go around. And as industry becomes more competitive, corporations see high quality people, people with skills and analytical minds, as necessary to excellence and competitive strength. They're going after those people, whether they are white, black, brown, red or yellow. So corporate America has to be concerned about education, and especially about a system that dumps millions of young people into an economy to which they can't contribute.

I've talked to dozens of corporate CEOs who tell me they are worried that there aren't enough skilled people in the work force, and that unless we improve the educational system their companies won't have the people they need. Last summer a group of top corporate CEOs rang some alarm bells about educational deficiencies. They came out with recommendations for massive new spending on education to cut the dropout rates and to improve academic achievement.

Now, that amounts to a new frontier of opportunity. For the first time in history, black people are in a position to enter the mainstream and to get the best jobs. But only if they measure up by objective standards, only if they have the right attitudes, skills, and education.

The fact is that too many of our kids can't make it in today's transition economy and don't have a hope of making it in tomorrow's high-tech economy. Black college entrance is down by ten percent in the past four years. The high school dropout rate is high. Many graduates don't have the minimum skills to hold a decent job. I should also add that the private sector has for too long used this terrible situation as an excuse, and not as the challenge it should be.

There are notable exceptions. The Urban League works with many employers to help recruit and train people for decent jobs. But too many employers don't want to become involved. And there are too many that cling to subtle, discriminatory practices that exclude minorities from responsible positions.

Yet, the future of corporate America will hinge on its willingness to make maximum use of our human resources, and that means hiring and training minorities for all aspects of corporate life. And it also means becoming involved in making the schools responsive to the needs and aspirations of all our young people.

Here in California, the business community has spearheaded education reform. You have made some progress. Don't stop now. Concentrate your efforts on increasing minority achievement, for true reform can't leave behind those most at risk.

Today, the school reform movement is on a roll; it's fashionable. But too much of it is off-base. Out of the dozens of school reform reports only a handful call for minority and community-based involvement. Many reformers think that if you tinker with a few requirements you've reformed the schools. You haven't. All you've done is ensure that minority kids will be pushed out faster.

And waiting in the wings are those who would destroy public education with a voucher system that would drain support and talent away from the public schools.

So we are now at a crossroads that will determine the shape of American education and the survival prospects for minority children.

That's why the Urban League movement will launch an education initiative in September, a movement-wide, planned, targeted effort with goals and timetables to improve black educational performance.

The time is ripe for an Urban League intervention to make the schools work for the children of the poor as they now work for the children of the affluent. The education initiative will be national in scope, as our affiliates frame programs based on models adaptable to local conditions. Some will modify current programs to develop greater accountability. Others will start from the ground up.

But all will be based on two firm pillars: advocacy and services. Advocacy will concentrate on making the schools responsive to the needs of black children. We will organize the community and build effective coalitions in support of quality educational experiences for minorities at risk. We will also provide direct services to students and their families—tutoring in math and science, counseling, dropout prevention—whatever model affiliates determine is best for their communities. Those services will be targeted and measured so that over a five-year period there will be significant results.

Ours is an accountable effort with defined goals and objectives that impact on the attitudes, performance and aspirations of our kids. We are trying to prevent another lost generation of black youth and we urge you to join us in this Education Initiative.

Business support is crucial to the success of efforts to build a quality educational system for all. The corporate community, no less than the minority community, has a major stake in enabling our young people to make it in this changing economy.

We Americans, and particularly the business community, need to become more aware of the importance of investing in our young people. They are the future—and unless we can give them a stake in our society they'll have no future and neither will we.

I'm reminded of the old Eddie Murphy film *Trading Places*. Perhaps you saw it, too. Eddie plays the part of a street hustler operating on the edge of the law until two rich men, playing a game of their own, put him in charge of a commodity trading business and give him a beautiful townhouse.

When they take him into that house, he starts pocketing the ashtrays. The men assure him that it is now his house. He can't believe them. "Do what you want," they tell him, "everything here belongs to you now." He crashes a valuable lamp to the floor. They just smile at him. "It's yours, do whatever you want." So Eddie brings his street pals to the house and they have a party. He sees them drinking his liquor, putting cigarettes out on his carpet, putting wet glasses on his furniture. He gets madder and madder, and finally throws them all out. "Look what they're doing to my house," he complains.

The moral is simple. Give people a stake in something, and they'll preserve it. They won't steal. They won't try to tear it down. When we give people opportunity, we give them a stake in the system. They become part of it; they contribute to it. Their lives are no longer desperate, but hopeful. Their energies no longer focus on simple survival, but on building for the future.

America was built on opportunity. Millions upon millions came to these shores, and are still coming, in search of opportunity. America's opportunities have to include the black poor who have been left behind in every great wave that moved the rest of us forward.

If America is to retain its greatness it must include those it has excluded; it must open windows of opportunity so that all of us have a stake in this land we have fought for and died for.

So let us work together to help build an America that lives up to its ideals:

An America that practices what it preaches and supports liberty for South Africa's black majority

An America that truly is a land of opportunity whose school system becomes an engine of mobility for the minority poor.

PUBLIC HIGHER EDUCATION AND BLACK AMERICANS:
TODAY'S CRISIS, TOMORROW'S DISASTER?[1]
CLIFTON R. WHARTON, JR.[2]

More than 16,000 participants—the largest number in five years—attended the 76th annual conference of the National Urban League held in San Francisco beginning on July 20, 1986. The civil rights organization, historically closely tied to corporate America, from which it received a large portion of its financing, has in recent years gradually sought to gain financial independence as it tackled issues that might not be popular with some of its supporters. According to the *Christian Science Monitor*, "In recent years Urban League has assumed a more activist posture and encouraged its members to seek coalitions with other civil rights organizations." (Luix Overbea, July 22, 1986, p. 5)

From the very outset, the new militancy of the organization was apparent. Indicative of the more activist role the league had begun to play was the opening keynote address of President John Jacob, which touched upon the issues of education, affirmative action, South Africa, and the status of Black Americans. According to the *New York Times*, Mr. Jacob delivered one of his strongest attacks ever on the Reagan Administration, its civil rights policies, and its policy of "constructive engagement toward the South African Government." (Lena Williams, July 21, 1986, p. 5) League members cheered National Association for the Advancement of Colored People (NAACP) executive director Benjamin L. Hooks, who urged greater cooperation among civil rights organizations, and hissed or walked out on a speech by Alan L. Keyes, a Black Reagan administration official, who urged restraint in the organization's demands for sanctions against South Africa.

It was in this highly charged atmosphere that Clifton R. Wharton, Jr. delivered a plenary address to the conference on July 21, 1986. Wharton, who is now chairman and chief executive officer of the Teachers Insurance and Annuity Association—College Retirement Equities Fund, was at the time of the speech chancellor of the 64-campus State University of New York system and chairman of the Rockefeller Foundation. He presented "an eloquent and compassionate speech" (National Urban League press release, July 21, 1986) entitled, "Public Higher Education and Black Americans: Today's Crisis, Tomorrow's Disaster?" Noting that Blacks have traditionally been "ardent believers in education as central to . . . bettering one's lot in life," Wharton addressed the question of whether Blacks are now experiencing "a crisis of faith in education as the privileged pathway to the future."

Dr. Wharton delivered his speech to an audience of approximately 3,000 delegates, members of the organization, business executives, and

---

[1]Delivered to the 76th annual conference of the National Urban League in the Moscone Center, San Francisco, at 2:30 P.M. on July 21, 1986.

[2]For biographical note, see Appendix.

media representatives at the Moscone Center in San Francisco at 2:30 P.M. on July 21, 1986. The speech received wide coverage in both local and national newspapers, as well as on television.

Clifton R. Wharton's speech: From our country's earliest colonial days, education has been the keystone to progress. Yet increasingly large numbers of American Blacks appear to be indifferent, apathetic, or cynical toward schooling and higher learning. Today, the question I'd like to ask is: Are we as Blacks experiencing a crisis of faith in education as the privileged pathway to the future?

Minorities in particular have been ardent believers in education as central to the uniquely American belief in bettering one's lot in life. It was no accident that made it a criminal offense to teach a Mississippi slave to read and write. Nor was it a coincidence that so many Black heroes during slavery were heroes of literacy, like Frederick Douglass. They realized that freeing their minds was the first and most important step toward freeing their people.

Since then, the quest for educational opportunity has been largely indistinguishable from the quest for freedom and justice. Education and equality, knowledge and power: more often than not, these goals have been one and the same for America's disenfranchised. They were one at the groundbreaking of Tuskegee Institute and Howard University. They were one and the same in Little Rock, and at Ole Miss, and at the University of Alabama. They have been one in Detroit, and in South Boston, and even in the lecture halls and anatomy labs of the School of Medicine of the University of California at Davis.

All this has been true to a greater or lesser degree for a vast cross section of Americans: working-class whites, women, the first waves of European immigrants, and later ones from Asia, the Middle East, and Latin America, and surely for almost every ethnic group that has sought to carve out a place for itself in our nation.

It has been especially true for Blacks, which may be another way of saying that if we cherished education more, needed it more, it was because the blanket of bigotry upon us was even coarser and more smothering than that cast over other groups.

And the struggle has been longer because our first ancestors came to these shores before the Mayflower!

For Blacks, increased access to education coincided with the advance of material progress and civil rights. Among the first triumphs was the rise of independent Black academies, technical training institutes, colleges, and professional schools. But in the South "separate but equal" placed a major constraint on achieving true quality and equality in our public schools. Jobs and education for their children were the dominant drives for those early Black migrants from the South to the North during the postreconstruction era and before World War I. Thus, until the end of World War II, Blacks participated with only limited success in this century's accelerating trend toward universal schooling.

Then, with the coming of the G.I. Bill, our pent-up demand for knowledge began to escape its confines, before being explosively released in 1954 with *Brown* v. *Topeka Board of Education*. The fraction of Blacks completing high school increased from 10 percent in 1940 to 70 percent in 1980. As late as 1965, Black enrollment in U.S. colleges and universities totaled only 274,000. By 1984, Black enrollment had multiplied nearly four times, to 1,138,000.

Until the 1960s, most of the growth in college enrollment took place on the campuses today called traditionally or historically Black. After that, the momentum of Black enrollment gains swung to the predominantly white, and especially the large public institutions. In 1960, about 96 percent of all Black college students were in 105 traditionally Black institutions; by 1984, the figure had fallen to 19 percent. Today, two-thirds of all Black college graduates receive their degrees from predominantly white campuses.

All this being the case, why are many other educators and I convinced that something has gone very, very wrong in education for Blacks, if not for other minorities? Why have I called it a crisis with disaster in the wings?

In recent years the pace of Black gains in education has fallen sharply and in many areas has reversed itself. The percentage of Blacks enrolling as full-time undergraduates peaked in 1978 at 10.6 percent. Thereafter there has been a gradual but steady drop each year. In 1984, the total enrollment of Blacks at all levels was a mere 8.8 percent.

What is going wrong? Well, for Blacks as well as others, the pool of college-age young people is shrinking—the "baby bust" it is called. But even though the "baby bust" is much less among Blacks and Hispanics than among any other group of 18- to 24-year-olds, our percentage participation rates in college are declining.

Next factor. The percentage of Black high school graduates who do go on to college has remained high, and roughly comparable to the figure for other segments of the population. For example, in 1980 the Black high school completion rate nationwide was about 70 percent, much better than a generation before, but still substantially lower than the 83 percent rate for white youth.

But these figures are cruelly deceptive, because they hide a profoundly negative factor: the obscenely high dropout rates in our schools. The overall 30 percent dropout rate for Black students nationwide soars to 40 percent, 50 percent, and even higher in many central cities. With these distressingly high rates little wonder that so many of the few who are left go on to college!

Dropping out among Black students starts as early as the primary grades and extends right through high school. In some urban areas, it has reached and passed crisis proportions. As for those who do graduate, many are academically underprepared as a result of attending classes in which keeping order has displaced rigorous instruction. Some students will have been automatically "tracked" into vocational rather than college preparatory programs, regardless of their aptitudes and abilities. Others still will have been programmed to blame themselves for the failures of the educational system and will have come to hate the very idea of further study.

So much for our high schools. Next, move up the educational ladder to the postsecondary level. How do we fare in our colleges and universities?

At the postsecondary level, the pool of Black youth eligible for college increased by nearly 20 percent during the last half of the 1970s, but the number who actually enrolled barely held steady.

As I mentioned a moment ago, the percentage of Black high school graduates who enroll in college is not much lower than for whites, but the dropout rate has so reduced the pool of high school graduates that Black young people participate in higher education well below our representation in the citizenry at large.

Once enrolled in college, Blacks are significantly less likely to complete a baccalaureate program than whites; dropping out does not end with the primary and secondary schools. Thus, the educational pipeline that was squeezed at the primary and secondary level is squeezed even further in college.

At the graduate and professional level, things look even worse. As early as 1976, the proportion of Blacks in graduate and first-professional programs had begun to fall from the already discouraging levels of the early 1970s. Although Blacks make up 12 percent of the U.S. population, they receive only about five percent of doctoral degrees annually.

What makes the situation gloomier still is that far too few Black graduate and professional students are going into the fields that promise the greatest opportunities for the decade ahead. In 1984, 1,049 Blacks in the U.S.A. received doctorates, but over two-thirds of them were in education and the social sciences. What about the high-demand fields? Listen to these national statistics: Blacks received 15 Ph.D.s in engineering, 13 in business administration, 11 in physics, 4 in mathematics, and 3 in computer science! With these numbers where do you think we'll get tomorrow's Black teachers and professors for our colleges and universities?

One last point, less frequently discussed: When the Black college enrollment is separated into male and female, a shocking picture emerges of even more massive enrollment declines for Black males. Black women already outnumber Black men on college campuses by a substantial margin. In New York, for example, Black females in 1983 received twice as many bachelor's degrees as Black males (5.3 percent to 2.7 percent). As someone who gazes out over the audience at several commencements every year, I can tell you that Black male graduates are starting to become an endangered species!

Well, what does it all mean?

Have we as a people lost our faith in education?

Don't we *believe* any more that schooling is the key that opens the locked doors, or if need be, the battering ram that knocks them aside?

Why, after having won at such terrible cost the right for our young people to attend school, has today's drop-out rate reached the point of being a national educational emergency?

After a sustained period of progress, why has Black college enrollment stalled or even begun to decline at virtually every level?

How will or can we correct for these massive losses in Black human capital, all those who were squeezed out of the educational pipeline?

Does the wider society realize the enormous cost and burden which it will ultimately pay by failing to avert the imminent disaster?

To me, these are deeply troubling questions. And many of the answers are just as troubling.

For one thing, there has been a major shift in public attitudes about equal opportunity, and especially about affirmative action. Not that long ago, there was a broad consensus about the nation's need for atonement to Blacks and other minorities by taking positive steps to reverse the harm inflicted by past abuse and lingering discrimination. Today, the National Urban League is one of the few remaining strong, biracial organizations. Meanwhile, the U.S. Attorney General and even some members of our national Civil Rights Commission offer up statements that would reverse decades of progressive thought and action.

Many of our fellow citizens seem to believe that the need for affirmative action is past.

That affirmative action has made inroads is clear to most of us. But it is also clear that 30 years of affirmative action has been barely a first step toward eliminating our country's 300 years of racism and discrimination. We need steps two, three, and four down the road toward full equality. And until we get there, the old vicious cycles will remain pretty much intact. Disenfranchisement breeds poverty breeds bad neighborhoods, which in turn breed bad schools and dropouts who can't get jobs. Unemployment breeds crime and welfare dependency and homelessness. Before long you're right back where you began. Only now you have a new generation seared with the permanent brand of oppression, locked permanently into what the sociologists have begun to call the "hard-core underclass."

Is there anyone here to whom this is news?

And yet I must say that there is a sense in which this analysis, so familiar and so intellectually comfortable, is nonetheless unsatisfactory.

It is only partially adequate to explain skyrocketing dropout rates and the erosion of Black gains in higher education. And it is unsatisfying because it raises the further question of why, two or three generations ago, Blacks somehow managed to advance educational goals even though the deck was stacked even more formidably against them.

The history of the National Urban League documents this. Many of you who are here today know that the barriers were much higher, the falls much harder—because you climbed the walls, you slipped and fell—and you rose to climb again! Whatever the remaining external, institutional barriers to education for Blacks today, they are on the whole fewer, and lower, than ever before. School integration is the law of the land. Overt discrimination in college admissions is practically unheard of. Even in its subtler forms, bigotry plays much less a part in the life of the typical campus than it did a short generation ago.

For the capable but underprepared, there are high school equivalency programs and developmental programs. For those economically in need, there are programs of financial assistance. Despite the hostile rhetoric of the current administration in Washington, the actual availability of federal financial aid has so far been only slightly curtailed. And while there is a growing barrier due to higher debt levels caused by more aid in the form of loans, the fact is that finances are seldom an insurmountable barrier.

Are persistent poverty and persistent discrimination obstacles to learning? Of course they are. Do delinquency, broken homes, alcohol and drugs, street culture, shoddy career counseling, youth unemployment, teenage pregnancy, and all the other enduring pathologies of disenfranchisement lie at the bottom of some of today's drop-out crisis and eroding college participation rates? No doubt about it.

But are they the root of the entire problem? That's another question, a harder, more complex, more intimidating question.

And, let's face it, a much touchier question. Touchier, because it may bring us face to face with other challenges, arising not altogether from discrimination, but at least in part from changes in the psychology and value system of the Black community itself.

Before continuing, let me make one thing quite clear. I have no use whatsoever for the current ideological fad that goes by the tag of "blaming the victim." I do not intend to claim that we as Blacks have become the source of our own problems. What I do want to suggest is that in education as in other important areas, Black problems have evolved into issues that cannot be resolved solely by traditional, institutional, "civil rights" approaches. And I want to argue that if that is indeed the case, we have an increasingly urgent obligation to explore additional, currently neglected avenues for change.

If you took a sample of Black college graduates from the 1920s, '30s, '40s, and '50s, you might be able to put together a kind of composite personality profile. I haven't done anything so systematic. But I have talked with and known more than a few of them. I've met them in business and industry, in politics and public service, in science and the arts. As a group, they form the backbone of faculty of today's traditionally Black campuses, and they are a smaller but vitally important presence in the faculties and administrations of our public schools and predominantly white colleges and universities.

Diverse as they are in so many ways, I've observed that Black college graduates from the '20s through the '50s tend to share several key psychological features.

They have a strong sense of self and heritage. They are family-oriented, and very often community-minded. They have tremendous drive and ambition. They know what they want to do. They know what they can do. They aren't much interested in all the reasons somebody tells them why it wasn't ever possible for a Black to do what they want to do. All they want to know is what it will take them to do it.

In a word, the Blacks who attended college in the '30s, '40s, and '50s were and are Blacks who *aspire,* and if their aspirations sometimes seemed unrealistic to an outside observer, well, he'd better just stand aside and watch. They knew they had to be twice as good as their white peers to compete successfully, but they had the self-confidence to respond to that challenge.

How does this compare with the situation facing today's Black college student?

On most college campuses we have a set of euphemisms. One is "educationally disadvantaged." Another is "academically underprepared." Yet another is "full-opportunity admit." By and large, these clumsy, unlovely phrases are almost universally interpreted to mean one thing. What they mean is "Black." The reverse is also true. Ask any faculty senate or administrative committee about Black students, and they will immediately begin to tell you more than you could possibly wish to know about special admissions tracks, free tutoring, developmental counseling, remedial reading labs, and all the other pedagogic paraphernalia associated with, not to put too fine a point on things, academic deficiency.

These views ignore that many Black students meet the same standards as all the rest without the slightest need for outside help or special dispensations.

They ignore that on most predominantly white campuses, nonminority students far outnumber the minorities in remedial classes. They ignore, in other words, the facts. No, the link between Blacks and deficiency is as unthinking, as reflexive as the link between deficiency and Blacks. It is a stereotype, but it is a stereotype that has taken on a life of its own.

It lives in the minds of many, perhaps even the majority of Americans.

It lives in the press. It lives in Hollywood and on the TV, where—"The Cosby Show" to the contrary—the story of Blacks is too often the story of an unwed, illiterate mother, a violent coke dealer, an abusive wife-beater, or a slightly buffoonish sidekick for a white superhero.

The stereotype also lives in the speeches of too many of our Black officials and political figures, for whom antidiscrimination and antipoverty programs are perennial issues, while industrial development and national trade competitiveness are somebody else's problem.

And most to the point for our discussion today, the stereotype is alive, and growing stronger every day, in the minds of our Black young people.

Through images, representations, the very structure of language, our society sends an overwhelming signal to today's Black youth. And the signal is: "Excellence is for the other folks. Not you." In one breath we decry Jensen's idiotic theories of Black intellectual inferiority; in the next breath we act as though he might be right.

I would like to be able to say that education is an exception to this corrosive assault, but it is not.

From the first day of the first grade, to the moment when the last strains of "Pomp and Circumstance" fade into silence, many and perhaps most of our schools, colleges, and graduate institutions beat the same dreary drum.

Start in kindergarten. Set up "slow" classes to homogenize the classrooms. Pass the "slow" kids anyway, whether they've learned the material or not. Just make sure they know they're getting by "because they're Black."

Design "aptitude tests" and academic tracking for the "culturally impoverished."

Hire guidance counselors who automatically, even benignly, steer Black youngsters away from college, toward jobs immediately after high school, or at best toward technical curricula leading to jobs with low ceilings of advancement.

Demand dual college admissions standards; better yet, lobby for a tacit but real lowering of academic standards for graduation, graduate school admission, and professional certification. And so on. And so on.

It is all reverse discrimination, in the only sense of that foolish phrase with any real meaning: discrimination by default, discrimination as the abdication of responsibility. And I must ask: Do we think that by these shabby devices we're doing Black youngsters a service? A *favor*? No. What we are doing is telling them, in a hundred whispered or unspoken ways each day, that we do not really believe in them. Is it any wonder so many of them are unable to believe in themselves?

It is hard to determine, and even harder to prove, just how thoroughly the individual's ability to compete, to excel, and to achieve are shaped by self-image, which is, of course, closely tied to the perceptions and expectations of the individual exhibited by others. But there is a large and growing body of empirical research data supporting the common-sense view that self-respect is critical to self-realization.

In a recent issue of *The New Republic,* two Black writers summed it up as follows:

. . . negative expectancy [among Black youth] first tends to generate failure through its impact on behavior, and then induces the individual to blame the failure on lack of ability. . . . This misattribution in turn becomes the basis for a new negative expectancy. By this process the individual, in effect, internalizes the low estimation originally held by others. . . . [This internal low expectation] powerfully affects future competitive behavior and future results.

Over the last several years, I have nursed a growing conviction that one of the most urgent needs for Black youngsters is a broad-based effort to foster stronger, more competitive, achievement-oriented self-images.

I must stress that the need is by no means universal. Studies undertaken by Professor Walter Allen at the University of Michigan show the other side of the coin. His 1982 survey of 902 Black undergraduates at eight predominantly white institutions found that the students did not fit the stereotypic profile. Indeed, they held high aspirations and strong self-esteem.

Sixty-three percent . . . expressed "above average" or "high" levels of self-confidence. Most students, 59%, thought they were above average or high in leadership abilities. And 76% said that overall they were high or above average people.

It takes only a moment's reflection to realize that these findings do not refute, but rather confirm my larger thesis. For the fact is that Professor Allen's respondents were *not* the high school dropouts, *not* the youngsters who never enrolled in college, but rather the self-selected successes: the survivors. Already admitted to institutions with formidable academic standards, they represented the survivors of a war of educational attrition. And not surprisingly, they succeeded because they had good high school records and came from stable, well-educated, middle-class families.

Such youngsters are thus the classic exceptions who prove the rule. But the majority of their peers, the majority of our young people, from kindergarten on, cry out for a massive infusion of self-esteem from our society as a whole, but most directly from the Black community itself.

There are a few areas where they already have it. Nobody needs to set up remedial programs to get Black kids into sports. In athletics, they know they can compete and even dominate. They see it for themselves, on every TV network. I'm not indulging in stereotype here for my own purposes. I'm trying to illustrate the effects of expectation on self-image and standards of performance. For unless you hold the dubious belief that Blacks as a group are innately and overwhelmingly superior to whites as athletes, you are forced to conclude that sports are a field we have excelled in because sports are a field we *believe* we can excel in. And our youth are willing to work long and grueling hours of practice and study so as to measure up!

Where is our comparable "intellectual competitiveness," our "intellectual work-ethic"?

I suspect that if you look carefully at the matter, you will find strong self-images and driving personal aspirations most deeply rooted in tight-knit, supportive, and—indeed, yes—demanding families.

Such families were a prominent part of Black America during the first half of this century. Their presence probably goes a long way toward explaining how those Black high school and college graduates of the '30s, '40s, and '50s could accomplish so much, even against such appalling odds. Recently many of us have begun to ask again about the role of the family and the critical importance of the values embodied in strong families: discipline, hard work, ambition, self-sacrifice, patience, and love.

It's easy enough to mock such values as bourgeois. But middle-class or not, they increasingly appear to constitute the spiritual foundation for achievement, the psychological infrastructure, if you will, for both personal growth and full participation in the world around us.

If you don't think such values are vital for intellectual growth, let me refer you to a recent study comparing the reading and mathematics skills of first and fifth graders in the United States (Minneapolis), Taiwan (Taipei) and Japan (Sendai). The sample included 1,400 students in the three countries. Its central finding was that the American students, who scored lower, did less homework, spent less time in school, and were more likely to engage in irrelevant, nonacademic activities while in class. But the study also noted the pivotal role of family values. American parents, it seems, now place less importance on homework and are less likely to push their children to achieve than parents in Japan and Taiwan. The researchers speculated that the old American "work-ethic" appears now to appeal more to Asians than to Americans themselves, at least insofar as it pertains to basic schooling. No wonder the newest Asian immigrant children are winning all the prizes!

Black gains in education and elsewhere have stalled at a time when the Black family as an institution has been under severe stress. I believe that is no coincidence. And so I must urge the rehabilitation of the Black family as an institution for the transmission of sound values.

It is difficult to know all that such a job entails, or how we might do it. But even given the reservoir of good faith and commitment that still exists among whites such as you who are here this afternoon, it is a job that the Black community must undertake largely for itself. It is a job that requires us to look mainly inward, to our own needs and potentials, rather than exclusively outward for assistance or reparations. And it is a job that calls for resources of creativity and strength that our own history documents in inspiring abundance.

Yet again, let me emphasize: I am not among that small group of Blacks who have gained recent attention for their indifference and even their disdain toward affirmative action and other forms of civil rights activism.

We have a full unfinished agenda covering the entire educational ladder. On one end, for example, we need to fight for per capita pupil expenditures in our Black inner cities which will at least equal those in our white suburbs. At the graduate end, we need many more programs like the recently announced $9 million program of the Ford Foundation to increase the pool of minority doctoral students.

The day for affirmative action is far from past. Realism compels us to recognize that it will be a long time before we have exhausted the need for legislative remedies to injustice and regulatory reform of institutions. Nor have we reached a point where we can, even if we wanted, move forward without our white compatriots' ongoing commitment. Yes, we need leaders and friends like David Kearns, Ralph Davidson, Coy Eklund, Bill LaMothe, John Akers and Don Keough. The help of thousands like them is essential if we are to achieve our ultimate goal.

But realism also compels us to recognize that for a growing segment of the Black population, despair has acquired a self-sustaining momentum. Welfare dependency, crime, unemployment, illegitimacy, and many other social pathologies arose initially from systematic disenfranchisement; today, they no longer require the negative energies of overt external discrimination to keep them running.

And to confront and reverse these pathologies, I am increasingly convinced that we need something new. We need strategies not to replace affirmative action and judicial activism, but to augment them.

While pressing the traditional lines of attack, we also need to open a second front.

We need to strengthen the Black family, particularly in communities where its structure and role have been progressively eroded over the last generation.

We need to reassert the relevance of self-respect and high aspiration, and we have to persuade Black youth that they can compete on equal terms not only in athletics and a few other circumscribed fields, but in fact across the whole spectrum of human striving, including intellectual.

Above all, we need to ask more of our own leadership. We have to call upon the growing cadre of Black leaders in business, labor, science, the arts, and education, as well as the traditional Black leaders in the churches and government. We must ask them to tell the country that the Black agenda is more than guarding Black "turf" or constantly repeating the litany of only Black issues.

In addition to national Black leaders, we need more national leaders who are Black. We need to remind our country that the war on poverty and discrimination is not just a Black issue, but an issue that directly affects the material and spiritual interest of every American. And we have to insist that the Black stake in America is a stake in the whole society. It is a stake in the full range of challenges and opportunities our country faces at the brink of the 21st century.

We need to open a second front, with a different set of strategies and tactics. The National Education Initiative adopted last year by the National Urban League represents a major opening volley on such a second front. I proudly congratulate John Jacob and the League for their nationwide crusade of educational renewal. Your five-year effort through your 113 affiliates harnessing each community's energies will prove to be a critical venture. I would particularly single out the League's "Math Count" program in Chicago because it seems to me very much a prototype of the kind of innovative, creative, and positive effort that offers a new kind of promise. It is a program that builds self-respect and nourishes high aspiration among our Black youth. It teaches them that they can compete and succeed. It aims at fostering skills and abilities that remove the ceiling to upward mobility in the society at large. But this is not the only program we should examine. There are others. This morning we heard of the outstanding efforts of Dr. Comer in New Haven and the CED program in Rochester. Each relies upon the only kind of resources and commitment that has never failed us—the resources and commitment of the Black community and its historic biracial coalitions such as the National Urban League.

Today's appalling school dropout rate and stalling of progress in higher education are only two aspects of what I believe to be an impending educational crisis for Black Americans. It is a crisis that may, as I have suggested in the title of my speech, be transformed all too soon into outright disaster.

And yet despite everything—despite the unexpected problems and reversals of progress, despite all the broken promises and heartbreaking setbacks—my counsel is not, finally, a counsel of despair. I recall Langston Hughes's famous, oft-quoted poem, "Mother to Son":

> Well, son, I'll tell you:
> Life for me ain't been no crystal stair.
> It's had tacks in it,
> and splinters
> and boards torn up,
> and places with no carpets on the floor—
> Bare.
> But all the time
> I'se been a-climbin' on,
> And reachin' landin's,
> And turnin' corners
> And sometimes goin' in the dark,
> Where there ain't been no light.
> So boy, don't you turn back
> Don't you set down on the steps.
> 'Cause you finds it's kinder hard.
> Don't you fall now—
> For I'se still goin', honey,
> I'se still climbin'
> And life for me ain't been no
> crystal stair.

It's been no crystal stair for any of us.

But for all the tacks and splinters and bare broken boards, we have reached one landing after another. We see the proof of our landings embodied in laws and institutions. We see them in our increased numbers in positions of prominence and influence. And we see them in matters less tangible, such as the strong, continuing support of enlightened white citizens for the National Urban League and other organizations devoted to justice and opportunity.

We've turned some corners, too. And it may be that we are turning another one, in asking ourselves whether we do not have an obligation to place the same high value as our fellow citizens on the fundamental American values of self-reliance and aspiration.

I said it before: again and again, the resources and commitment that have never failed us have always been those of the Black community itself. They are rooted in an enduring faith that we can overcome, we can achieve our goal of full equality.

In the final analysis, we are the ones who can and who must eradicate the insulting and infinitely destructive equation our society continues to make between Blackness and inferiority. We are the ones who can and who must reassert the Black claim on excellence, for our young people, no less than for ourselves.

After all the years of climbing, we know the weariness all too well. But we also know the perils of sitting down to rest. And in these darkening years of our century's close, there are times when the illumination of truth and compassion seems to have flickered or even failed.

Must it be that we will have to light our own way? If so, let our lamp be the lamp of learning, and let it burn brighter today than yesterday, and brighter tomorrow than today.

THE HISPANICIZATION OF THE UNITED STATES[1]
PAUL SIMON[2]

During 1986 and 1987, Central America was often in the headlines in American newspapers and frequently was a leading subject on the evening television news. Two separate, but not unrelated, developments contributed to this attention. One was the increase in the number of illegal aliens entering this country from Central America, and the second was the clash between Congress and President Ronald Reagan over foreign policy in that area, especially over aid to military forces trying to overthrow the government in Nicaragua.

As early as February, 1986, the Commission of the Immigration and Naturalization Service warned that there had been a "startling" surge of illegal aliens entering the United States from Mexico and Central Ameri-

[1]Delivered to the Commonwealth Club of California in San Francisco on February 13, 1987 at a noon luncheon in a banquet room of the Sheraton Palace Hotel.
[2]For biographical note, see Appendix.

ca. "We are seeing the greatest surge of people in history across our southern border," Commissioner Alan C. Wilson said, explaining that economic trouble in Mexico and Central America was largely responsible for the growing number of persons illegally entering the United States. (*New York Times,* February 21, 1986, p. 1) No one, at the time, knew how many illegal aliens were already living in this country. In an effort to identify and protect illegal aliens now residing here, Congress subsequently enacted legislation conferring legal status, or amnesty, on those who have lived continuously in the United States since January 1, 1982, a program described as "the largest legalization of illegal immigrants ever undertaken by any country." (Robert Reinhold, *New York Times,* May 7, 1987, p. 8)

In addition to the problem of illegal aliens, American involvement in Nicaragua erupted into national headlines with the discovery later in 1986 that members of the National Security Council, in contravention of Congressional acts expressly forbidding military aid to the "Contra" rebels, had secretly been supplying them with funds. Adding to the sensational aspects of the disclosure was the revelation that funds for payments to the rebels had, in part, come from the profits of secret sales of arms to Iran in return for the release of Americans being held captive by terrorists. This development led to the appointment of special prosecutors and investigating committees.

Senator Paul Simon addressed the issues of Latin American foreign policy and domestic immigration problems in a speech to the Commonwealth Club of San Francisco on February 13, 1987. He titled his talk, "Hispanicization of the United States: How It Is Affected by the Situation in Central America." Simon, who served ten years as a member of the House of Representatives before being elected United States Senator from Illinois in 1986, pointed out:

> The United States admits more legal immigrants than all other nations combined. We are rightfully proud of this. But sensible limitations and their effective enforcement are essential to the stability and growth of our country.

The Senator then suggested seven steps that he felt would promote "a sensible handling of today's and tomorrow's immigration problems and opportunities."

Senator Alan Cranston inserted Simon's speech into the *Congressional Record,* observing that the speaker

> . . . offered some enlightening insights into the relationship between U.S. policy in Central America and some of the immigration questions and issues that confront my state and the nation. . . . [In the address he] brought his experience as a member of the Senate Subcommittee on Immigration and Refugee Policy and years of thoughtful analysis of our relations with our neighbors to the south to bear upon the subject. (March 18, 1987, p. S3431)

Just over three months after delivering this speech, on May 18, 1987, Senator Simon announced that he would enter the race for the 1988

Democratic presidential nomination. Commenting on his announcement, columnist Jeff Greenfield wrote:

> At 58, Simon is the oldest Democrat in the race; he is also most obviously a candidate shaped in the Pre-Television Age. His haircut comes courtesy of Pop's barbershop, not the $40 coiffeurist's. His glasses—not contact lenses, but glasses—suggest a CPA rather than a fighter pilot. And he not only wears bow ties, but seems determined to adopt that symbol of antiquated formality as his campaign symbol. The supreme irony about all this is that these symbols of old-fashioned Norman Rockwell simplicity could not have been more shrewdly designed for our times had they been a product of a multimillion-dollar p.r. campaign. As it happens, these visible symbols of simplicity may in fact be the perfect "image" for our times. (Baton Rouge *State-Times*, May 22, 1987, p. 8B)

Senator Simon presented his address as the final keynote address of a two-day conference on "Rehispanicization of California?" organized by the Commonwealth Club of California. The 84-year-old educational group has 16,000 members, most of whom are business executives, financiers, educators, lawyers, and students. His audience consisted of 350 members and guests attending a noon luncheon meeting at a ballroom in the Sheraton Palace Hotel in San Francisco on February 13, 1987.

Paul Simon's speech: Fellow Immigrants:

California and the nation face a problem caused by immigration, but not a problem unique in the annals of American history nor unique in the history of California. The usually wise and thoughtful Benjamin Franklin, in 1753, warned about Germans coming into Pennsylvania, calling them "the most stupid of their own nation." He noted that since they do not speak English we "cannot address them either from the press or pulpit; it is almost impossible to remove any prejudices they may entertain. . . . Not being used to liberty, they know not how to make modest use of it." Franklin feared that German-speaking people would soon out-number the English-speaking "and even our government will become precarious."

Does all of that have a familiar ring to it?

In 1846, the governor of California, then under Mexican rule, saw progress in California "threatened by hordes of Yankee emigrants."

A century ago, many Californians and Americans were worried about what they called "the yellow peril," the immigration of Chinese into the United States and, particularly, California. Anti-Chinese rallies were held in this state. The prestigious club, Native Sons of the Golden West, was determined that the 31st star in the flag "shall never become dim or yellow."

Americans have always been writing to their House and Senate members complaining about immigrants. Resentment against the Irish led to "Irish Need Not Apply" signs in much of the nation. West European Jews complained about East European Jews coming in. The 1892 Democratic national platform read: "We heartily approve all legitimate efforts to prevent the United States from being used as the dumping ground for the known criminals and professional paupers of Europe." Animosity toward Japanese-Americans and Japanese immigrants during World War II led to one of the most disgraceful actions in the history of the federal government. Floridians have complained about "the Cuban invasion," and Californians have complained about the numbers from Southeast Asia and Mexico. Much of all of this is simply history repeating itself. And those complained about will contribute greatly to the nation, just as those who preceded us, and were the objects of scorn, did. But some things are different.

When your grandparents complained about the Chinese immigration, the national population was 50 million in 1880, compared to 227 million in 1980. In 1880, the population of California was 800,000; and in 1980, it was 24 million. A century ago, the population of Mexico was 12 million, and today it is 80 million.

The rate of population growth in California will slow, but the make-up of the population is projected to change fairly dramatically. In 1980, 66.5 percent of California's population was non-Hispanic and white, and 50 years from now it is projected to be 38.4 percent. In 1980, blacks comprised 7.5 percent of the population, and 50 years from now they are projected to be 6.7 percent of the population. In 1980, Asians comprised 5.6 percent of the population, and in the next 50 years that figure is projected to grow to 15.6 percent, the highest percentage growth of any ethnic group. Fifty years from now the Vietnamese will be the largest Asian community in California, with the Filipinos second. The Hispanic population is projected to grow from 19.2 percent of California's population in 1980 to 38.1 percent in 50 years. Proximity to Mexico is the major reason for the growth of the Hispanic population in the southwestern United States. But cultural factors are present also. Even the names of cities are more comfortable: San Francisco, San Jose, Los Angeles have a more familiar ring than Springfield, Decatur and Peoria.

One factor has changed dramatically since the days when your grandparents came to the United States. When a Swedish citizen came here in the year 1900, five of our states had not been admitted to the union. We were still a somewhat primitive nation with huge areas of land almost untouched. That Swede who came over in 1900 had only a third-grade education. But he had a strong back and the will to get going. And—most significantly— there were plenty of jobs available for the unskilled. The United States of 1987 is dramatically different, with approximately 10 million people unemployed and the demand for unskilled labor declining.

The dominant concern in immigration for California and the nation is the Hispanic immigration. Because of your proximity to Mexico and Central America, you have a greater concern on this issue than most states. And with the flow of immigrants there are problems that have to be addressed.

You are the nation's most urban state, and many of the immigrants who will reach your state and our nation are not accustomed to urban life. A myth that has grown up around those who have entered this nation illegally for jobs is that they primarily work in agriculture. Actually, less than 20 percent enter farm work. Urban assimilation of a non-urban people makes your problem more difficult. California has approximately one million who are here illegally, undocumented workers who often are exploited and frequently fear defending themselves legally or moving ahead too far economically, frightened by the specter of exposure and deportation.

One-fourth of the foreign-born living in the United States today are in California. Almost one-third of the foreign-born Hispanics live in your state, and approximately 40 percent of the foreign-born Asian-Americans live in California.

Many of these people compete with those born here for jobs, particularly jobs that require limited skills. That can create ethnic tensions along with economic problems.

Population growth in California for the decade 1970 to 1980 was 18.5 percent, the smallest in your state's history. In two decades of your history, you have had growth over 60 percent; in three decades, over 50 percent; and in four decades, growth over 40 percent. The projected growth that you face in numbers is not that awesome. The projected growth for this decade is slightly less than the previous decade, and that growth continues to decline under these projections to 7.2 percent growth four decades ahead.

But those projections are just that: projections. And while the new immigration law, in theory, might slow that growth, there are other unknowns that could change these figures dramatically. One is Mexico's population and economic outlook, and the second is the prospect of peace and economic growth in Central America.

Mexico's population will roughly double in the next 40 years. If, on top of that, Mexico should have more serious economic problems—and that is no remote possibility—the projected immigration figures in California will change dramatically.

If Central America's economic problems are compounded by serious financial woes, repressive regimes, and an escalating conflict, the present flow of legal and illegal immigrants to this nation from that area will increase substantially.

The United States admits more legal immigrants than all other nations combined. We are rightfully proud of this. But sensible limitations and their effective enforcement are essential to the stability and growth of our country. We now admit far fewer, relative to our total population, than we have admitted for most of our history, roughly one-fifth as many in this decade as in the decade 1900–1910. From time to time we change our quotas. My amendment, now law, to increase the quota from Hong Kong grew out of the specific problems that colony faces. The Italian foreign minister spoke to me the other day about a change he feels is needed in our immigration laws. I am checking that out. There will be modifications in our law from time to time. But the basic law is sound, and we did the right thing last year to eliminate the inconsistency of saying to an immigrant, "You cannot legally work here," but at the same time saying to an employer, "It is perfectly legal to hire these people." That employer magnet will gradually lose its power.

The United States was a largely empty nation when George Washington wrote, "The bosom of America is open to receive not only the opulent and respectable stranger, but the oppressed and persecuted of all nations and religions." We are no longer an empty nation, but the spirit of Washington's statement is still with us and, I hope, always will be. We are able to welcome more than most nations but not in unlimited numbers. And we have some problems.

What can we do to promote a sensible handling of today's and tomorrow's immigration problems and opportunities?

Let me suggest seven steps that are not earth-shakingly new, but sometimes we ignore the obvious:

1. We must work with Mexico to improve the economy of our neighbor to the South.

Some observers have noted with considerable accuracy that the United States is bounded by two countries, one we do not regard as a foreign country, and one which we ignore.

Ignoring Mexico's problems is folly. It invites political extremism next to our borders. It avoids the reality that a less prosperous Mexico makes more likely a less prosperous United States. And it ignores the population factors that would cause great stress between our two countries.

If there should be more severe economic problems in Mexico, or if there should be political upheaval and a repressive dictatorship as a result of these problems, we could pass a dozen sweeping immigration bills, build a fence 30 feet high all along the 1,900 miles of that border, and employ 10 times as many border patrol officials; and despite all these measures, the massive stream of people into the United States would be unlike anything we have ever witnessed. Would we turn a cold shoulder to these desperate people? Occasionally, we have ignored the world's desperate, and we have always been ashamed of our conduct later. Usually, we have responded in a humanitarian way.

The right answer is to work cooperatively with Mexico *now* to encourage so much that is good in that country. Economic disaster can be avoided, but it is by no means a certainty that it will be. Mexico must become more than an after-thought in a politician's speech.

2. In Central America, the United States should listen to our neighbors south of us who are virtually unanimous in publicly saying that our policies in that area are short-sighted, hurting the cause of democracy, and an encouragement to extreme elements.

Our friends are right, and our policy is wrong. And that flawed policy has caused more than half a million Central Americans to enter our country as undocumented workers. That number could grow dramatically.

When foreign policy is built upon passion rather than reason, upon impulse rather than thoughtfulness, it is usually wrong.

Well over a year ago, I was asked to speak to a group of educators gathered from various nations in Washington. Before I began my remarks, I asked if there were any Nicaraguans in the audience. Two men raised their hands, and I said I wanted to speak to them afterwards. I asked both of them, "What should the United States be doing in Nicaragua?" Both said that they were opposed to the Sandinistas but added, "Let us solve our own problems. Don't send down your weapons that are killing us." Where will we be one year from now if we approve the latest request for $105 million in weapons for the Contras? Where we are today—but with approximately 6,000 more Nicaraguans killed by U.S. weapons, and U.S. policy further discredited around the world. If we decide that we should overthrow every government we do not like, that is about two-thirds of the governments on the face of the earth. Our hands would be full.

Does that mean that we abandon Nicaragua to the Marxists? The oldest and most solid democracy in Central America is Costa Rica. A few weeks ago, the president of Costa Rica was in Washington and told two of us, "I denounced the Sandinistas at the United Nations, the only head of state to do so other than President Reagan. But the weapons you are sending down to the Contras make constructive change in Nicaragua less likely, and it is destabilizing to the other democracies in that region, including Costa Rica." General Paul Gorman, in charge of U.S. forces in that area, recently told a congressional committee that the Contras are not likely to win, no matter how much money we provide. And the lesson of Vietnam should be clear: If we supply weapons to people, but the cause they espouse does not have a popular base, that cause will fail. The people of Nicaragua may not be in love with the Sandinistas, but the evidence is strong that the Contras are less popular. The Contras do not control a single village or city in Nicaragua. They are primarily based in Honduras, where we have quietly also created a permanent base, and the presence of both the Nicaraguan Contra force and the U.S. armed forces are destabilizing to probably the best government Honduras has ever had. There are other ways to fight Marxism in that area of the world.

For example, the United States today provides approximately 3,400 scholarships for Central American students who want to go to college in the United States. Cuba and the Soviet Union provide approximately 8,900 scholarships. My own strong impression is that if we were to provide more scholarships and fewer weapons, the cause of democracy would be much strengthened in Central America.

Those who would attempt to topple the Sandinistas through supply of weapons to the Contras usually have a view of the developing world that is about 20 years old. They see a wave of new leaders in developing nations moving toward Marxism. That was true two or three decades ago, but most of these leaders have become disillusioned with that dream and are much more pragmatic today. It does not put them automatically in the camp of the West, but it does mean that subservience to any nation is a thing of the past. If we show with our concern and our example that a free system can provide answers, they will move toward freedom.

The growth of democratic institutions in all areas of the world is one of the non-headline-producing realities that Jefferson and Madison and Lincoln would applaud. We should encourage free institutions, economic development, and peace in Central America. To the extent that we ignore any of the three, we aggravate U.S. immigration problems.

3. Civil libertarians, immigration and law enforcement officials, and concerned citizens should discuss what can be done to solve the problem of an identification card. Almost all nations have one, and every study on the enforcement of immigration laws collides with this problem. Many Americans believe the idea of having an identification card smacks of a police state. Are there ways to solve the problem, perhaps through the issuance of a voluntary identification card for those who want it? I don't have the answer. All I know is that every study on the immigration problem runs into this dilemma.

4. We should step up efforts to find an inexpensive way of converting salt water to fresh water. The question is not whether that inexpensive method will be found, but when. If one percent of the present defense budget were devoted to this research, the contribution to the security of this nation and to the enrichment of humanity would be beyond measure. It would be of great assistance to California and the southwestern United States, to much of Africa and to the troubled Middle East; and significantly for the topic of the day, it would be of great help to the economy of Mexico, relieving the pressure to emigrate dramatically. A breakthrough is not imminent, but what is now a non-priority should become one.

5. A sensible jobs program that, in a fairly sweeping way, overhauls our present welfare and unemployment compensation system, is needed for both those born in the United States and for our new citizens. We are not going to let people starve within our borders, so we face the choice of paying people for being productive or non-productive. That should not be a difficult choice. Legislation I will be introducing soon would move us in the right direction, assisting not only the less fortunate, but making the nation more productive and relieving economic pressures on states like California.

6. Efforts to assist immigrants to acquire English language proficiency need to be strengthened. The zealots who banned the teaching of German in schools during World War I were as wrong as the anti-foreign-language Know Nothings of the 1850s or those who passed legislation prohibiting Chinese translations in our courts. The recent passage of English as an official language referendum in your state is, at best, meaningless and has its roots in these similar efforts over the years. Unfounded fears about language separatism are as old as this nation, and analogies to Canada or Belgium are without accuracy because in our country, the pattern is for Germans or Poles or Hispanics or Italians or Chinese to cling to each other geographically and culturally for a time and then, eventually, follow the same paths to the suburbs and to assimilation. But immigrants who cannot speak or read or write English are at a greater handicap than they would have been a century ago. Assimilation is retarded. If the same effort that is now put into fear-filled campaigns against the non-English-speaking were directed toward more English classes and further educational and skill development, everyone would benefit. Virtually all immigrants want to learn English, but many do not have that opportunity. And the answer is not simplistic solutions like dropping bilingual education. Bilingual education is needed for many students as a bridge until competence and confidence is developed in English skills. Young and old need to have available to them practical learning opportunities for English language development. Our failure to do more is harmful to immigrants and harmful to the development of a more productive nation, guided by informed citizens.

Finally, we must recognize that the different cultural backgrounds others bring to our shores provide an opportunity for cultural enrichment. The United States reflects our rich heritage in many ways. On Main Street America you will find Chinese and Greek restaurants; you can buy tacos and Polish sausage and crepes and wienerschnitzel and pizza and shishkebab and chicken curry and sushi and borscht and barbecued ribs and McDonald's hamburgers. But it is not only our stomachs that should learn the rich diversity that is America. Our minds must learn that also. And immigrants can help teach us. As we learn Spanish and Chinese and other languages and as we learn about other cultures, we will develop markets in other countries. For the reality is: You can buy in any language, but if you want to sell, you must speak the language of your customer. As we read and listen and learn, our lives will be enriched. Too often we pass by the opportunity to learn from these unpolished gems in our midst. That is a loss to our new neighbors and a loss to each of us and to our country. Cultural provincialism has been the cause of many of our nation's well-intentioned blunders.

Immigration presents both problems and opportunities. But the simple gestures of friendship, both to our new neighbors and to the nations from which they came, will bring rewards beyond calculation.

MYTHS, HEROES, AND IMPERTINENT QUESTIONS

OF MERMAIDS AND MAGNIFICENCE[1]
JOHN SILBER[2]

On May 18, 1986, John Silber, President of Boston University, delivered the 113th commencement address. In impromptu remarks preceding his prepared address, Dr. Silber observed:

> Fifteen years ago I arrived here, without roots in Boston. I had roots, but they had been left in my native state, which as some of you may know, is Texas. I did not feel a stranger in Boston—no one with a sense of American history can ever feel a stranger in Boston—but neither did I feel at home. Today I find myself very much at home in Boston and rooted in the history of this university. I am honored to be addressing the class of 1986 on my fifteenth anniversary.

Contrary to an editorial in the *Daily Free Press*, the Boston University student newspaper, Silber was in no danger of fading quietly into the dustbin of history. Dispute and controversy had marked his tenure at Boston University almost from the onset. He has been called "articulate" and "pugnacious." (*New York Times,* November 9, 1981, p. 10) In 1980, a writer for *People* magazine summed up his reputation as follows:

> Among faculty members and students alike, opinion is bitterly divided as to whether Silber is a colossus who has rescued BU from mediocrity or a megalomanic who has shattered its spirit. He is far and away the most controversial college executive in the country today. (June 2, 1980)

In spite of his controversiality, Silber is recognized as a national spokesman for higher education.

In his commencement address, Silber announced that his subject was "the place of the hero in a democratic society." He maintained that although democracy "places the highest value upon the development of the individual," it paradoxically is "frequently indifferent to heroes and hostile to greatness. . . . Yet democracies, like all human societies, need heroes and require a vision of greatness if they are to achieve their potential." In developing his theme, Silber drew heavily upon his Texan background, as well as his knowledge of Greek philosophy and English literature.

Silber delivered the commencement address at Nickerson Field, the university athletic stadium, late in the morning on May 18, 1986, to an

---

[1]Delivered at the commencement exercises of Boston University at Nickerson Field in Boston, Massachusetts, late in the morning of May 18, 1986.
[2]For biographical note, see Appendix.

audience of 4,998 graduates and approximately 10,000 parents, friends, and faculty. His address was preceded by the awarding of degrees and honorary degrees.

John Silber's speech: This commencement marks the fifteenth anniversary of my inauguration as seventh president of Boston University. By contemporary standards, my fifteen years as president have brought me almost to the threshold of venerability, within striking range of such epithets as "kindly old President Silber." Indeed, in the last issue of this year's *Daily Free Press,* an editorial consigned me to the dustbin of history with the words: "the long afternoons seem to be fading quietly into the twilight of John Silber's tenure at Boston University."

Fifteen years ago I arrived here, without roots in Boston. I had roots, but they had been left in my native state, which, as some of you may know, is Texas. I did not feel a stranger in Boston—no one with a sense of American history can ever feel a stranger in Boston—but neither did I feel at home. Today I find myself very much at home in Boston and rooted in the history of this University. I am honored to be addressing the class of 1986 on my fifteenth anniversary.

My subject is the place of the hero in a democratic society. It is a striking paradox that democracy places the highest value upon the development of the individual, yet is frequently indifferent to heroes and hostile to greatness. Alexis de Tocqueville, observing the American scene in the 1830s and 1840s, devoted a chapter of *Democracy in America* to the extreme scarcity of lofty ambitions among otherwise intensely ambitious Americans.

Moreover, in a vigorous democracy there is a natural and praiseworthy skepticism among free people when they are confronted by those with heroic ambitions, above all when their ambitions tend towards the dictatorial.

Yet democracies, like all human societies, and indeed like all individuals, need heroes and require a vision of greatness if they are to achieve their potential. The Athenian poet Aristophanes has his chorus praise Athena, the presiding goddess of that democratic city-state: "Thou great aristocrat: make this people noble. Help us to excel." True excellence, the poet suggests, is accessible to all, not merely to those of noble lineage. It is essential to American democracy, no less than it was to Athenian democracy, to reconcile greatness of soul with liberty and equality.

To some extent our backgrounds shape our ideas about how greatness and equality are to be reconciled. My own were molded by my Texas origins and by the role of the hero in Texas culture. Consider the fall of the Alamo, a story which is part history, part legend, and perhaps part myth. New light has been shed on it by the great actor, Peter Ustinov.

He was asked by a Texan how he liked making "Viva Max," a fantasy on the re-taking of the Alamo by the Mexican army. He remembered, he said, a meeting with Governor Preston Smith of Texas. The Governor ritually re-told how the leader of the Texans, Colonel Travis, had drawn his sword, cut a line across the dirt floor, and voiced his famous challenge: "All who choose to fight and die for Texas' independence, cross over and stand with me."

And Governor Smith concluded, and at that point Ustinov developed a rich Texas accent—"'Every Texan crossed over that line with Colonel Travis.'"

"But Governor," Ustinov asked, "If all those in the Alamo crossed the line and stayed, and if they all died with Colonel Travis, how is it that we know the story?"

The Governor was undaunted: "Mr. Ustinov, that's because a French feller named Rose refused to cross the line; he turned tail and ran. But he weren't no Texan."

"Ah," said Ustinov, "Would he perhaps be the one who inspired that famous song, "The Yellow Rose of Texas?"

This yarn did nothing to diminish the glory of our heroes; nor did a famous incident during John F. Kennedy's presidential campaign of 1960. After a stunning speech to a large, enthusiastic crowd assembled in front of the Alamo, Kennedy wanted to make a quick exit. Turning to Maury Maverick, a local politician and a great-great-grandson of Sam Maverick of Boston who fought at Bunker Hill, he said: "Maury, let's get out of here. Where's the back door?" "Senator," said Maury, "if there'd been a back door to the Alamo, there wouldn't have been any heroes!"

More seriously, we may wonder about the accepted account of the fall of the Alamo. Conceivably, we owe our account of the heroes of the Alamo to the Yellow Rose of Texas, but this seems unlikely. Rose would hardly have talked. Who then was the anonymous poet, the blind Texas Homer of the tale? Who composed this epic event, whose end no one ever witnessed? What other source could there be than the fact that the defenders, outnumbered some 20 to 1, were prepared to give their lives for freedom—that they, like Patrick Henry, set a higher value on liberty than on life? The less poetic interpretation—that the defenders were just too stupid to leave—had limited appeal in those parts.

The story of the Alamo, as we now have it, provides a rational and satisfying account of an otherwise inexplicable event. It also provides us with democratic heroes who are satisfyingly manageable: heroism is more tolerable in the dead, since the dead no longer constitute a threat to the living.

But heroism has never been merely consigned to the graveyard, or to public statues of our honored dead. Educational institutions—in all societies, from the simplest to our own—have considered courage as a virtue and the hero as exemplary, an ideal to be emulated. The philosopher Alfred North Whitehead has argued that moral education depends upon our recognition of the essential role of heroes in life: "The sense of greatness," he wrote, "is the groundwork of morals." A surprising statement, for Whitehead is claiming that morality, which establishes the norms for action, is grounded in an appreciation of greatness, which, by transcending the norm, intensifies one's motivation to attain it. Whitehead then proceeds: "Moral education is a fundamental education of the whole self into action or being. This is impossible apart from the habitual vision of greatness."

And this sense of greatness, he held, must be embodied in myth or story, rather than in some catalogue of moral virtues or duties held up for us to strive toward. "The sense of greatness is an immediate intuition and not the conclusion of an argument." The story of the brave defense of the Alamo is a more powerful image of moral greatness than any to be obtained by a course in ethical theory. It is an essential and traditional function of literature and art to provide these immediate intuitions of greatness, hence the great role assigned to literature and art in liberal education.

Simply recall how liberal education has fulfilled this function in the past. Documents from the Boston school system a century ago make it clear that the inculcation of the heroic life was crucial to the curriculum: Macaulay's *Lays of Ancient Rome,* Milton's *Paradise Lost,* and Scott's *Ivanhoe* were studied in high school. Grammar schools assigned reading in the history of England and the United States, in which such figures as Henry V, Queen Elizabeth, Sir Walter Raleigh, Washington, Lincoln and Jefferson were held up to the young as models to be emulated.

In *McGuffey's Readers,* the dominant textbooks of American education in the nineteenth century, the emphasis is less dramatic but no less edifying. The heroic is domesticated, and brought within the purview of the child: greatness becomes accessible. Examples of Roman generals, European kings, queens, and knights are therefore rare. The greatness is of smaller scale, but its relevance has been widened, democratized. A prudent, honest, confident George Washington, a steadfast, compassionate Lincoln—these appear in the company of wise grandmothers, sacrificing parents and good children. The moral impulse behind *McGuffey's Readers* is the same as that which produced a sign on the wall of the San Antonio YMCA when I was a boy: "Don't wait to be a great man. Be a great boy!"

Unfortunately for us and our age, our educational system has become less and less effective in transmitting our birthright of heroism, our patents of potential nobility. With the tragic disappearance of the idea that there are certain books that every educated person should read (the *Bible,* the *Iliad,* the *Dialogues* of Plato, to mention only three), we have lost that idea of inspiriting greatness of which Whitehead speaks. The heroes of the *Iliad* display the realities of human existence, the basic modalities: the importance of learning from life—of ripening, the meaning of excellence, the nature of friendship, the necessity of loyalty and courage, the tragic solitude of our condition and the inevitability of death.

None of this is now a part of the common experience—the common curriculum—of high school graduates. This means that many lack the texts of their potential humanity, even their spiritual survival. They will all face, surely before they are thirty or forty, the loss of close friends or a family member, the loss of love, disappointed hopes. Ignorant of the heroes of ancient Greece, ignorant of Biblical heroes, ignorant of greatness, they will not know David's lament on the death of Jonathan:

The beauty of Israel is slain upon thy high places;
  how are the mighty fallen!
From the blood of the slain, from the fat of the mighty,
  the bow of Jonathan turned not back,
  and the sword of Saul returned not empty.
Saul and Jonathan were lovely and pleasant in their lives,
  and in their death they were not divided:
They were swifter than eagles, they were
  stronger than lions.
Ye daughters of Israel, weep over Saul,

who clothed you in scarlet, with other delights,
who put on ornaments of gold upon your apparel.
How are the mighty fallen in the midst of the battle!
O Jonathan, thou wast slain in thine high places.
I am distressed for thee, my brother Jonathan:
very pleasant hast thou been unto me;
thy love to me was wonderful,
passing the love of women.
How are the mighty fallen,
and the weapons of war perished!

Magnificent. Had Achilles heard it, he might well have said: "These words would have graced the death of Patroclus." Achilles could not hear those words; we can. We can, but do not. And lacking these texts of greatness, we may then find ourselves dumb when we most need to articulate our grief, deprived of the company of those who have suffered greatly before us and like us.

But our need for exemplars is not limited to coping with grief or the other modalities of human life. There is also need for greatness in community and national life. But this need does not ensure the emergence of heroes in a democratic society, nor does it overcome the ambivalence that citizens in a democracy feel about heroes and heroism.

The fundamental obstacle to the emergence of political heroes is found in the electoral process itself. If the people are to be led by heroes, the people will have to elect them. Every American politician knows that foremost among his tasks is pleasing a majority of his constituents.

But what are the consequences of trying to please everyone? Alexis de Tocqueville thought he had found the answer. In December, 1831, he noted in the diary of his American journey that "When the right of suffrage is universal, and when the deputies are paid by the state, it is singular how low and far wrong the people can go."

Several days later, traveling on a steamboat, he met a man who had left his wife, gone to live among the Indians, taken an Indian wife and liked to take a drink. When he heard that this man was also a former government official, who, like Huck Finn, had lit out for the territory, Tocqueville believed he had found proof that the people can go low and far wrong indeed:

We are traveling at this moment with an individual named Mr. Houston. . . . This man was once Governor of Tennessee. . . . I asked what could have recommended him to the choice of the people. His having come from the people, they told me, and risen "by his own exertions." . . . They assured me that in the new western states the people generally made very poor selections. Full of pride and ignorance, the electors want to be represented by people of their own kind. . . . [To get elected,] you have to haunt the taverns and dispute with the populace.

But Tocqueville was soon forced to reappraise the wisdom of the backwoods Jacksonians who had elected Sam Houston Governor of Tennessee and would, a few years later, elect him the first President of the Republic of Texas. Fascinated by this man of the people, Tocqueville questioned Houston about his life among the Indians, and before long he was taking pages of notes on their religion, their government, their concepts of justice and the role of Indian women. Then the conversation turned to an analysis of U.S. government policy toward the Indians, and again Tocqueville took pages of notes.

When it comes time to sum up his impression of Sam Houston, Tocqueville no longer sneers, but is sympathetic and, finally, deeply impressed by this man of the people. He writes: "The disappointments and labors . . . that have accompanied his existence have as yet left only a light trace on his features. Everything in his person indicates physical and moral energy."

Sam Houston is one type of the democratic hero: ambitious, large-spirited, driven by a personal code of honor, in touch with the people and with the land, a friend to the indigenous peoples, but a pioneer in promoting civilization in their territories. But it is surely worth remembering that Houston, honored as a genuine hero, died an outcast, despised by his fellow Texans for opposing Texas' secession from the Union. Houston and other heroes have found that doing the right thing is seldom popular and often fails to achieve success in any obvious sense. Indeed, having a clear recognition of this fact, the unpopularity of opposing the popular, is one of the traits that defines the hero—especially in a democracy.

In September, 1960, Dr. Frances Oldham Kelsey, an official of the Food and Drug Administration responsible for the approval of new drugs, received an application for a new sedative called thalidomide. Although the manufacturer pressed again and again for quick approval, Dr. Kelsey withheld it because she found the testing incomplete. This led to accusations that she libeled the manufacturer. After a year of intense pressure on Dr. Kelsey, the manufacturer conceded that the drug had been withdrawn from sale in West Germany. Incredibly, he continued to press the application. Dr. Kelsey held firm. By March, 1962, the association of thalidomide with birth abnormalities was clear, and the manufacturer finally withdrew the application. As a result of her heroism, this country was spared the birth of perhaps thousands of seriously deformed infants. Europe, lacking similar heroes in its bureaucracies, was not spared.

But even if there were never opposition to heroes and even if heroes did not need to be courageous, problems would nevertheless arise. For in the confrontation of greatness with the ordinary, we can glimpse what might be called the shadow of the hero. I can perhaps best define what I mean here by briefly analyzing the effects of the hero. On the one hand, he exalts and motivates; on the other, he intimidates and demeans. That this problem is particularly difficult in a democracy was recognized in Pericles' Funeral Oration. Pericles speaks to the relatives of those who died defending Athens:

> But for those of you here who are sons and brothers of these men, I see a great conflict awaiting you. For the dead are always praised; and you, even were you to attain to surpassing virtues, will have a hard time being thought of—not as their equals, but even as men slightly inferior.

Under the rubric of the heroic shadow, I group several intimidating or negative aspects of greatness in the democratic hero. Among these are, above all, resentment—the way in which greatness evokes envy and rancor among those less great and the way in which it misleadingly absolves others of their responsibilities; the way in which it discourages future generations; and by no means least of all, the way in which greatness may be expressed in great evil.

Such villains as Iago, Tamburlaine and Milton's Satan, Richard III and Lady Macbeth are themselves perverse heroes, evil heroes. However wrongly, however terribly, they *act*.

There are also those who, from within a culture, achieve an understanding or an approach to life which challenges what that culture considers heroic: Job, for instance, refusing to accept the arguments of his comforters; or Hamlet, a man whose excessive self-consciousness makes him unable to act, a prototypical hero of that elevated consciousness in which " . . . the native hue of resolution/Is sicklied o'er with the pale cast of thought."

But in our time, perhaps the most far-reaching effect of the heroic shadow is the figure of the anti-hero. We have all seen him. There are several species of anti-hero: some are repelled both by the idea of greatness and by those who exemplify it. Others are frightened by greatness; still others, bored. All these anti-heroes shared a conviction that heroism is not for them, but rather an ambition, a fate to be avoided.

Perhaps the best literary portrait of the anti-hero is Prufrock in Eliot's poem, "The Love Song of J. Alfred Prufrock." A weak, sensitive and timid man, but conscious of heroism in human life, he occasionally contemplates doing something that might, for him, amount to an heroic act—but he always sinks back, with an ironic sigh, into passivity.

No! I am not Prince Hamlet, nor was meant to be;
Am an attendant lord, one that will do
To swell a progress, start a scene or two . . .

Prufrock knows there is an "overwhelming question," but asks us not to ask it and instead, in his stream of consciousness, we find a portrait of the failing society which, he is convinced, has no use for serious questions. He is, when all is said and done, a man conversing with himself, alone. His final realization is the fading of his life and his approaching death. Not daring to disturb the universe, he draws back from the seductive forces of life which beckon the hero:

I grow old, I grow old.
I shall wear the bottom of my trousers rolled.
Do I dare to eat a peach?
I shall wear white flannel trousers,
  and walk upon the beach.
I have heard the mermaids singing, each to each.
I do not think that they will sing to me.

The mermaids sang to Achilles and to David, to Sam Houston and Kelsey; and, terrible as their song may have been, the mermaids also sang to Stalin and to Lucrezia Borgia. With a certain self-pity and resignation, the anti-hero says sadly: "I do not think that they will sing to me."

The tragedy of Prufrock and those like him is that the mermaids may in fact be singing to them, but they are simply incapable of hearing the song. This is a tragedy for them personally; it means that they are forever prisoners of the impotence of irony. But it is an even greater tragedy for our democratic society which must have leadership in order to survive.

There is truth, of course, in what Prufrock felt. How does an individual, aware of his limits, of his mortality, achieve that sense of greatness that is the motivating force of life?

Regrettably for us all, the question is more apt to be avoided than answered. The most common means of avoiding it is to abandon consciousness altogether in the mindless pursuit of pleasure. In thrall to hedonism, cut off from past and future, a disconnected present is all that remains of human life. Even when hedonism is pursued as Don Giovanni pursues it, with cosmic intensity, it betrays the final emptiness of the anti-hero. The poverty and paucity of meaning negate any notion of the heroic.

Another method of avoiding consciousness of the problem is deliberate denial of individuality. The denier feels no envy of the heroic personality; he is beyond the shadow of any individual greatness. I am speaking of the "Marxist hero": he renounces all claim to, indeed all belief in, individual effort or worth; he finds his place within the historical dialectic. History for him is made not by individuals, but by dialectical forces operating through social classes. He submerges himself, not only *accepting* his destiny as an obscure member of society, but *seeking* this obscurity as his fulfillment. In the words of the Marxist theorist, Plekhanov:

He not only serves as an instrument of necessity and cannot help doing so, but he passionately desires this, and cannot help desiring to do so. This is an aspect of freedom.

Orwell could not have invented a finer example of doublethink.

But for those who refuse to abandon either consciousness or individuality, who thus reject the nostrums of hedonism and Marxism, the problem of the heroic remains and must be confronted. The democratic man in his ordinariness must find that sense of greatness on which moral achievement depends. If he is not motivated by greatness in the abstract, he must be able to appropriate for himself a relevant model like Jefferson, whose greatness includes a refinement and a reach which to some seems beyond that of the common man; or a man like Sam Houston, whose greatness was expressed not only in heroic appetite, ambition, and achievement, but in a magnanimity and a common touch that endeared him to Indians, Mexicans, blacks, frontiersmen, and French aristocrats; or a woman like Dr. Kelsey, who finds opportunities for heroic courage in the midst of bureaucratic detail.

The proper response of the individual to greatness is that each person should emulate the great. Such emulation, it will be said, is incompatible with the notion of individualism. Goethe best answers the charge:

Gleich sei keiner dem andern; doch gleich sei jeder dem Höchsten.
(Let none be like any other; but let each be like the Highest.)

But the democratic hero remains, as he must, a paradox. For
all their greatness, Jefferson, Houston and the heroes of the Alamo, like all other men, were subject to the "discourtesy of
death"—the ultimate democracy. The democratic hero, however
great, shares the mortality and limitation that attend all human
endeavor. He lives not only in the great light of his significance—
of which he may, like Sophocles' heroes, be unconscious, though
we are not—but in the stark realization of his insignificance.

This duality is eloquent in the great chorus of Sophocles'
Antigone, which emphasizes both the brevity of man's life and the
glory of his accomplishments on earth:

Numberless are the world's wonders, but none
More wonderful than man; the stormgray sea
Yields to his prows, the huge crests bear him high;
Earth, holy and inexhaustible, is graven
With shining furrows where his plows have gone
Year after year, the timeless labors of stallions.
Words also, and thoughts as rapid as air
He fashions to his good use; statecraft is his,
And his the skill that deflects the arrows of snow,
The spears of winter rain; from every wind
He has made himself secure—from all but one:
In the late wind of death he cannot stand.

It reaches us from the Bible, where the Psalmist notes man's
insignificance:

As for man, his days are like grass; as a flower of the field, so he flouri-
sheth.
For the wind passeth over it, and it is gone; and the place thereof shall
know it no more.

And another Psalmist responds by proclaiming man's glory:

What is man, that thou art mindful of him?
And the son of man, that thou visitest him?
For thou hast made him a little lower than the angels,
And thou hast crowned him with glory and honor.
Thou madest him to have dominion over the
    works of thy hands.
Thou has put all things under his feet.

It reaches us from the Gospel of Mark, where Jesus tells his fol-
lowers that in the kingdom of heaven "many that are first shall
be last and the last first"—and, from the same Gospel:

There came one running, and kneeled to him and asked him, "Good Master, what shall I do that I may inherit eternal life?"
And Jesus said unto him, "Why callest thou me good? There is none good but one, that is God."

This humility, the humility of Jesus as true man, is balanced by the claim in John's Gospel of Jesus as true God.

The Christian paradox offers perhaps the profoundest expression of this union of incompatibles. In its terms, we are to be at once humbler than the lowest, and exalted by our share in the life of God. Jesus, "very God and very man," as the *Book of Common Prayer* has it, unites these opposites, reconciles human mortality and divine greatness. The least of men may be the Christian hero. There has never been a more democratic conception.

This paradox confronts not only ancient Greeks and characters from the Bible, but also twentieth-century Americans. It confronts us in the climax of Arthur Miller's *Death of a Salesman*—a play that a Yale professor told me could not be a tragedy, because tragedies had to do with heroes, and Willy Loman was just an ordinary fellow who failed because he was a bad salesman. Yet for Miller the life and death of a salesman is worthy of the highest art. It is about us, and we should not be ashamed to read it and to weep honest tears of self-recognition.

We find ourselves voicing both sides of that climactic scene between Willy Loman and his son, Biff, where Biff, out of a life of failure, tells his father:

"Pop! I'm a dime a dozen and so are you!"

And Willy replies:

"I am not a dime a dozen! I am Willy Loman and you are Biff Loman!"

Then Biff, at the peak of his fury:

"Pop, I'm nothing! I'm nothing, Pop! Can't you understand that?"

Biff collapses in tears, and Willy says:

"What're you doing? What're you doing?"

He turns to his wife, and asks:

"Why is he crying? . . . Isn't that remarkable? Biff—he likes me! . . . He . . . cried to me."

Then Willy, choking with his love, cries out his promise:

"That boy—That boy is going to be magnificent!"

We do not have to choose between Biff and Willy. Both are right. They are a dime a dozen and they are magnificent. The fact about human beings is that we are both a dime a dozen and we are magnificent. If we believe only that we are magnificent, we become insufferably arrogant at best, and Tamburlaines at worst. On the other hand if we believe that we are merely a dime a dozen, we lose our reason for being, the motivation for excellence and the ability to sustain the disappointments and losses that go with even the happiest and most fortunate of lives. Heroism is not only essential to democracy, it is also essential to the life of every human being. The genius of democracy is found in this paradox: that we are all a dime a dozen and that we are all magnificent.

The democratic hero is not an ideal beyond our grasp; it is relevant and compelling to each of us.

We know from looking about us that wisdom is within the reach of anyone, for some of the simplest human beings are wise. Virtue is within the reach of anyone, for some of the least educated are good. Happiness is within the reach of anyone, for some of the poorest are happy. There is neither a positive nor a negative correlation between intelligence, learning, and wealth on the one hand and wisdom, virtue, and happiness on the other.

The mermaids sing each to each, and they sing to each of us. But not all of us hear their song.

Why should we resign ourselves to insignificance and forfeit our promise of greatness? Unless, in the words of Augie March, the protagonist in Saul Bellow's novel, "you want to say that we're at the dwarf end of all times, and mere children whose only share in grandeur is like a boy's share in fairy tale kings, beings of a different kind from times better and stronger than ours."

The class of 1986 should affirm that they do not live at the dwarf end of time, that heroism is not the stuff of fairy tales, that our times can be better and stronger than the past. This affirmation requires courage to live while confronting the ultimate indignity of death. But that ultimate defeat does not rob us of the possibility of victory in life. Only by the loss of nerve do we forfeit victory.

I am confident that the class of 1986 will not forfeit the victory that is yours for the daring.

Let us stand in the tradition of our heroes ancient and modern. Facing the certainty of the worst, we can respond to the challenge of the best:

Of course we are all a dime a dozen.
And we are all magnificent.

THE VALUE OF IMPERTINENT QUESTIONS[1]
GARRY TRUDEAU[2]

In 1974, for the first time in the history of the awards, the Pulitzer Prize for cartooning went to a noneditorial-page artist. The recipient was Garry Trudeau, creator of *Doonesbury*, a comic strip. The strip, which originally had a small cult following, caught the imagination of the public and by 1975 appeared in more than 400 newspapers, with a readership of 40 million. Veteran satirical columnist Art Buchwald has called *Doonesbury* "not only the best comic strip, but the best satire that's come along in a long time," and Meryle Secrest of the *Washington Post* has noted Trudeau's "wry, pertinent, and sometimes savage humor, his political acumen, his tolerance for minority groups . . . [and] his ability to represent the viewpoint of a young, educated, and disenchanted audience." (*Current Biography*, 1975, p. 420)

Doonesbury had its origins in a comic strip which Trudeau did for the Yale University *Daily News* as an undergraduate. It was then and remains today a very popular feature of college papers. When later, under the aegis of Universal Press Syndicate, thirty newspapers (including the *Washington Post*) began to carry it, some conservative editors dropped it. Trudeau explains why: "It is usually understood by both reader and editor that the comics are a special kind of territory, the sacred part of the paper, unantagonizing, unconfronting, almost tranquilizing. It is the one place in the newspaper where a man can find predictable, often mindless entertainment. This is the way many readers like it and this is the way many editors keep it." (*Current Biography*, 1975, p. 421) In denying this traditional expectation by commenting on current events and public figures in an exaggerated and admittedly tendentious manner, Trudeau frequently has exasperated both readers and publishers.

In view of his popularity with college students, his selection as the commencement speaker for Vassar College's 123d commencement exercises on May 25, 1986, is not surprising. Further, Vassar had set a precedent when they invited humorist Art Buchwald to deliver the commencement address in 1975.

In his address, Trudeau urged the graduating class to adopt a healthy skepticism and to learn to ask impertinent questions. Specifically, he urged the audience to question the rationale of the Strategic Defense Initiative (also known as Star Wars defense) as a matter of "simple duty." He said that 6,500 college scientists, including a majority of professors in 109

---

[1]Delivered at the Vassar College commencement exercises at an outdoor, natural amphitheatre overlooking Sunset Lake on the campus in Poughkeepsie, New York, at 10:00 A.M., May 25, 1986.

[2]For biographical note, see Appendix.

university physics and engineering departments, have declared they would not work on the project because they believe it to be "ill-conceived and dangerous."

In the speech, Trudeau combined humor and good-natured skepticism with outspoken opposition to a major policy proposal of the government. Unlike many commencement speakers, Trudeau took advantage of the invitation to address the graduates to make a statement on an important national issue.

Trudeau delivered his address to an audience of approximately 3,500, which included 560 members of the class of 1986, their families, Vassar faculty, administrators, and alumni, and people from the Poughkeepsie, New York, community. The ceremony, which began at 10:00 A.M., was held at an outdoor, natural amphitheatre overlooking Sunset Lake on the Vassar campus.

Garry Trudeau's speech: Ladies and gentlemen of Vassar:

My wife, who works in television, told me recently that a typical interview on her show used to run 10 minutes. It now runs only five minutes, which is still triple the length of the average television news story. The average pop recording these days lasts around three minutes, or, about the time it takes to read a story in *People* magazine. The stories in *USA Today* take so little time to read that they're known in the business as "News McNuggets."

Now, the average comic strip only takes about 10 seconds to digest, but if you read every strip published in the *Washington Post*, as the President of the United States claims to, it takes roughly eight minutes a day, which means, a quick computation reveals, that the Leader of the Free World has spent a total of 11 days, 3 hours and 40 minutes of his presidency reading the comics. This fact, along with nuclear meltdown, are easily two of the most frightening thoughts of our times.

There's one exception to this relentless compression of time in modern life. That's right—the graduation speech. When it comes to graduation speeches, it is generally conceded that time—a generous dollop of time—is of the essence. This is because the chief function of the graduation speaker has always been to prevent graduating seniors from being released into the real world before they've been properly sedated. Like all anesthetics, graduation speeches take time to kick in, so I'm going to ask you to bear with me for about a quarter of an hour. It will go faster if you think of it as the equivalent of four videos.

I want to speak to you today about questions. About pertinent questions and impertinent questions. And where you might expect them to lead you.

I first learned about pertinent questions from my father, a retired physician who sued to practice medicine in the Adirondacks. Like all parents racing against the clock to civilize their children, my father sought to instruct me in the ways of separating wheat from chaff, of asking sensible questions designed to yield useful answers. That is the way a diagnostician thinks. Fortunately for me, his own practical experience frequently contradicted his worthiest intentions.

Here's a case in point: A man once turned up in my father's office complaining of an ulcer. My father asked the pertinent question. Was there some undue stress, he inquired, that might be causing the man to digest his stomach? The patient, who was married, thought about it for a moment and then allowed that he had a girlfriend in Syracuse, and that twice a week he'd been driving an old pick-up down to see her. Since the pick-up frequently broke down, he was often late in getting home, and he had to devise fabulous stories to tell his wife. My father, compassionately but sternly, told the man he had to make a hard decision about his personal priorities if he was ever to get well.

The patient nodded and went away, and six months later came back completely cured, a new man. My father congratulated him and then delicately inquired if he'd made some change in his life.

The man replied, "Yup. Got me a new pick-up."

So the pertinent question sometimes yields the impertinent answer. In spite of himself, my father ended up teaching me that an unexpected or inconvenient truth is often the price of honest inquiry. Of course, you presumably wouldn't be here if you didn't already know that. I'm confident that your education has been fairly studded with pertinent questions yielding impertinent answers.

But how many of you have learned to turn that around—to ask the impertinent question to get at that which is pertinent?

I first came across the impertinent question in the writings of that master inquisitor, Studs Terkel. He himself claims to have adopted it from the physicist Jacob Bronowski, who once told him, "Until you ask an impertinent question of nature, you do not get a pertinent answer. Great answers in nature are always hidden in the questions. When Einstein in 1905 questioned the assumption held for three hundred years that time is a given, he asked one of the great impertinent questions: 'Why? How do I know that my time is the same as yours?'"

The impertinent question is the glory and the engine of human inquiry. Copernicus asked it and shook the foundations of Renaissance Europe. Darwin asked it and is repudiated to this day. Thomas Jefferson asked it and was so invigorated by it that he declared it an inalienable right.

Daniel Defoe asked it and invented the novel. James Joyce asked it and reinvented the novel, which was promptly banned.

Nietzsche asked it and inspired Picasso, who restated it and inspired a revolution of aesthetics.

The Wright brothers asked it and their achievement was ignored for five years. Steven Jobs asked it and was ignored for five minutes, which was still long enough for him to make $200 million.

Whether revered or reviled in their lifetimes, history's movers framed their questions in ways that were entirely disrespectful of conventional wisdom. Civilization has always advanced in the shimmering wake of its discontents. As the writer Tristan Vox put it, "Doubt is precisely what makes a culture grow. How many of what we call our classics were conceived as the breaking of laws, exercises in subversion, as the expression of doubts about the self and society that could no longer be contained?"

The value of the impertinent question should be self-evident to Americans, for at no time in human history has it been asked more persistently and to greater effect than during the course of the American experiment. It is at the very core of our political and cultural character as a people, and we owe our vitality to its constant renewal.

Today, the need for that spirit of renewal has never seemed more pressing. There is a persistent feeling in this country that many of our institutions have not measured up, that with all our resources and technology and good intentions, we as a nation are still a long way from fulfilling our own expectations. The social programs that have failed to eliminate poverty, an educational system which has seen its effectiveness seriously eroded, the chemical breakthroughs that now threaten man's environment, the exploding booster rockets, malfunctioning nuclear power plants—these are but some of the images that have shaken our confidence. According to a recent poll, the only American institution that still enjoys the trust of a majority of college students today is medicine; only 44% of those polled trust educational institutions, 29% trust the White House, 23% trust the press and only 21% say they trust religion.

It's difficult to think of an institution in this country that has not had to re-examine its agenda, to ask impertinent questions about the purpose and the means of its mission. Society's leaders, whose number you join today, face a wall of public cynicism. As professionals, they have to speak more clearly about what they *can* do. As citizens, they have to speak clearly about what they *should* do.

Nowhere is the need for accountability more urgent than in what is shaping up to be the largest coordinated national undertaking of your generation—the Strategic Defense Initiative. It may well become the most fiercely contended issue of your times. Already 6,500 college scientists, including a majority of professors in 109 university physics and engineering departments, have declared their opposition to SDI and have signed a "pledge of non-participation" in a project they have called "ill-conceived and dangerous." The group, including 15 Nobel Prize winners, maintains that the weapons system is inherently destabilizing and that further pursuit of its development is likely to initiate a massive new arms competition.

The actions of these scientists constitute an extraordinary repudiation of the amorality of indiscriminate weapons research. Science, since it leads to knowledge, has all too frequently led its practitioners to believe that it is inherently self-justifying, that there is nothing dangerous about splitting atoms in a moral vacuum. These attitudes are held in abundance by some of the brightest people of your generation, who are already hard at work on what nearly *all* of them concede is a dangerous fantasy.

Listen to these comments from the young Star Warriors still in their 20s working on particle beams and brain bombs at Lawrence Livermore National Laboratory:

This from the inventor of the atomic powered x-ray laser, "Until 1980 or so, I didn't want to have anything to do with nuclear anything. Back in those days I thought there was something fundamentally evil about weapons. Now I see it as an interesting physics problem."

His co-worker, another brilliant young physicist, says he has doubts about the wisdom of SDI but concurs that "the science is *very* interesting."

A third member of the team had this to say: "I think that the great majority of the lab's technical people view the President's (Star Wars) speech as somewhat off the wall and the programs being proposed as being, in the end, intrinsically rather foolish. But obviously, the lab is benefiting right now and will continue to benefit, and everybody's happy with the marvelous new work."

Marvelous new work, indeed. As a TRW recruiting brochure put it recently, "We're standing on the first rung of a defense development that will dominate the industry for the next 20 years." Why? Because weapons manufacturers think Star Wars will work? On the contrary, at a recent trade show, McDonnell Douglas boasted on one wall its Star Wars hardware while on a facing wall, it displayed proposed Star Wars countermeasures, including a "maneuvering re-entry vehicle" and a "defense suppression vehicle." GA Technologies is already marketing the latest in "survivable materials" to protect American missiles from a *Soviet* defensive system.

No one in the defense industry seriously believes in a "peace shield"; in fact they're betting against it. If an American SDI is big business, then the hardware needed to overcome the anticipated Soviet response is even bigger business. The industry is further encouraged by the mindless momentum of the program, as evidenced by the recent admission of Reagan's undersecretary of defense that he pulled the $26 billion price tag out of the air.

Said the official, "I tried to figure out what the hell we're talking about. [Congress] wanted a number and kept on insisting on having a number. OK. First year was $2.4 billion, and I figure, OK, best we could handle is maybe a 20%–25% growth."

Little wonder that during the program's first year, the money could not be spent fast enough to use up the yearly appropriation. Undeterred, the following year the administration asked for $2.5 billion, greater than its request for all the basic research financed by the National Science Foundation and Department of Energy combined.

It should not surprise us that so many in the scientific establishment find this obscene. Said computer scientist David Parnas, who recently quit an SDI advisory panel, "Most of the money spent will be wasted; we wouldn't trust the system even if we did build it. It is our duty . . . to reply that we have no technological magic (that will make nuclear weapons obsolete). The President and the public should know that."

To question the rationale of the SDI enterprise should be, as Mr. Parnas suggests, a question of simple duty. It shouldn't have to be an impertinent question, but that's exactly what it's becoming. The Star Wars juggernaut may already be unstoppable. $69 billion dollars will be spent by 1994. A representative of Hughes Aircraft recently predicted, "By 1988, it may be institutionalized." Lobbies are already being mobilized, interests are becoming entrenched, foreign governments are already being involved, on the sound theory that Star Wars will be harder to stop if it becomes part of Allied diplomacy. And all around the country, some of the most talented men and women of your generation are being recruited to solve "an interesting physics problem."

The impertinent question. We need it now more than ever.

And yet, sadly, healthy skepticism is at odds with the prevailing sentiment of our times. As Tristan Vox sees it, "arguments abound to the effect that a nation does not grow great by doubting itself, indeed the self-criticism was the trap that American democracy had laid for American greatness."

We've been here before. It was called the '50s. This supposedly conservative doctrine holds that the very qualities from which this country has traditionally drawn its strength—idealism, openness, freedom of expression—are naive and dangerous in a cold war struggle. It maintains that America's raucous squabbles, our noisy dissent—in short, its very heritage—have weakened us as a nation and caused it to lose its unchallenged supremacy.

As the *New Republic*'s Mike Kinsley put it, "Talk about blaming America first."

In such an atmosphere, the impertinent question comes with risks. Ask the two engineers at Morton Thiokol who protested the launch of the doomed Challenger space shuttle. Ask any Pentagon procurement whistle-blower. Ask David Stockman. The mere fact of this president's widespread popularity casts suspicions on the motives of even the loyalest of oppositions. There is, of course, no question that this president seems to have fulfilled a deep yearning in many Americans to feel positively about their country. And yet, the Reagan presidency often reminds me of a remark made by a woman to sportscaster Heywood Broun following the victories of the great racehorse Secretariat in the Triple Crown. After the trauma of Vietnam and Watergate, she told Broun, Secretariat had "restored her faith in mankind."

I would submit to you that Ronald Reagan is the Secretariat of the '80s. He has restored our faith in ourselves, and for that, we are all in his debt. It does not, however, exempt his administration from criticism from concerned citizens who love their nation as much as he does. One of the things that has always distinguished this country from most others is that we've always challenged ourselves to do better. As a satirist, I can't foresee any administration, Republican or Democratic, under which the basic message wouldn't be the same—that it's possible to do better.

This is the true glory of America. This hope is what stirs me as a patriot—not a winning medal count at the Olympics, not the ability to drop 9,000 servicemen on a Caribbean golf course, not jingoistic commercials that tell me that the pride is back, America, when for many of us the pride never left, and certainly not by the fantasy of 1,000 laser rays criss-crossing the heavens in software-orchestrated precision, obliterating a swarm of supersonic projectiles.

Skeptical? You bet. You're looking at a man who has attended 16 graduations, at four of which, including one technical college, the microphone failed.

The impertinent question. The means by which we reaffirm our noblest impulses as a people. But what about the impertinent question as it pertains to us as individuals? Bronowski had an addendum to his comments on the subject. "Ask the same kind of question," he charged Studs Terkel, "not about the outside, but the inside world; not about facts but about the self."

This is impertinence of the gravest sort. The inner life finds very little currency in this, the age of hustle. David Stockman has written of a leadership circle which is intellectually inert, obsessed by television, bored by introspection and ideas of substance. Meanwhile, all across town, the sad stories of sleaze abound, 110 to date, all pointing the new prevailing ethic of corner-cutting and self-advancement, whose only caveat is the admonition not to get caught.

It can seem a pretty grim picture. Indeed, as you look around you, you see very little to distract you from this narrow path. And yet that is exactly what your liberal education—with its emphasis on ideas, on inquiry, on humanist values—sought to do. As the president of my alma mater once observed, "The whole point of your education has been to urge you to see and feel about the connectedness among things and how that connectedness must be fostered so that civilization is sustained."

Our understanding of the interdependencies of the human experience is the only force which keeps a society from fragmenting. The extent to which you seek that understanding is the extent to which you will be strong enough to repudiate the callousness you see around you.

This won't please you, but let me share a little of what one of the more astute voices of your generation, 24-year-old David Leavitt, has written about his peers: "Mine is a generation perfectly willing to admit its contemptible qualities. But our contempt is self-congratulatory. The buzz in the background, every minute of our lives, is that detached ironic voice telling us: At least you're not faking it, as they did, at least you're not pretending as they did. It's okay to be selfish as long as you're up-front about it."

This is a pretty bleak portrait of the values of a generation, and my guess is I'm staring at hundreds of exceptions. My further guess is that the yearning for moral commitment is as intense as it always was, but that the generation with no rules, the generation that grew up in the rubble of smashed idealism, fallen heroes and broken marriages is deeply suspicious.

Columnist Ellen Goodman has speculated that this is why apartheid and the soup kitchen have emerged as the causes of choice; they offer that stark unambiguous clarity that World War II offered their grandparents, that sense that there is no good news about the other side of the argument. But Goodman, being incorrigibly of her era, also believes that micro evolves into macro; that to be involved inevitably leads to decisions between imperfect options; that many of you will take risks, make mistakes, and become citizens in spite of yourselves.

I'm afraid there's simply no other way. If ours becomes a society intolerant of failure and uncompassionate in the face of suffering, then surely we are lost. With the uncertainties of the future hedging in on you, you need to assess your commonalities. You need to say how you would treat other people, and how you would have them treat you back.

The best your college education can do for you now is to remind you that it's one thing to be self-absorbed and quite another to be self-aware. It comes down to a matter of being open, of seeing. It comes down to a matter of remaining intrigued enough by life to welcome its constant renewal. In short, it comes down to the impertinent question.

From those of us floundering out here in the real world, to those of you preparing to enter it, may I just say, welcome. We need you.

Thank you and good luck.

- - - - - - -

EDUCATION: MYTHS AND MORALS[1]
PATTI P. GILLESPIE[2]

- - - - - - -

Throughout most of this country's history, Americans have been concerned with the quality of education afforded our young people. From time to time, this concern has exploded into controversy, as when in 1957 the Soviet Union launched a rocket into the sky, causing many to conclude that the United States had fallen behind in the space race because of an inadequate school system, and again in 1983–84 when a series of studies completed by several prestigious commissions reported a 20-year decline in student examination scores and unfavorably compared American students with their peers in other countries.

In the ensuing examination of American education, the public and media focused most attention on the surveys, statistical studies, and parental complaints while giving scant attention to those most directly concerned with educating students: the teachers.

In a speech to a conference of two regional speech communication associations on April 9, 1987, a teacher and university administrator reflected on her own background and experiences to discuss what she regarded as three widely accepted myths about education and the morals to be drawn from them. The speaker was Dr. Patti P. Gillespie, president of the Speech Communication Association and chairman of the Speech Communication Department at the University of Maryland. Her audience was approximately 150 members of the Southern Speech Communication Association and the Central States Speech Association at a general session of their joint convention in St. Louis. She delivered the address in the Meramec room of the Clarion Hotel at 5:00 P.M. on April 9, 1987.

Basing most of her conclusions on personal experience, Dr. Gillespie organized her address around what she called three myths: (1) Education is a commodity, and students are consumers; (2) Education is about answers, not questions; (3) Bigger is better. Debunking these myths, Gillespie proposed an educational system that emphasized inquiry over pat answers, learning as "not a destination but a journey," and quality over size. She went on to note that her proposal would not be popular "because it turns education into a personally upsetting, even threatening activity."

Patti P. Gillespie's speech: When I was elected two years ago, Jane Blankenship told me that the best part of being SCA [Speech Communication Association] president was the chance to travel

- - - - - - -

[1]Delivered at a general session of the joint convention of the Southern Speech Communication Association and the Central States Speech Association in the Meramec room of the Clarion Hotel, St. Louis, Missouri, at 5:00 P.M., April 9, 1987.
[2]For biographical note, see Appendix.

about the country giving epideictic addresses. I have learned quickly, if painfully, that I do not share Dr. Blankenship's gift for the epideictic. My situation has been further complicated by the fact that my research areas are at some distance from yours: I work in theatre's theory and history, fields that are increasingly distant from even the most generous definition of communication. And because I lacked both John Bowers' wit and his infinite connections, I couldn't offer an expose of people whom I had known in SCA.

Indeed, I had begun to feel a rising sense of panic about a suitable subject when help came from a most unlikely source, William Bennett, whose continuing pronouncements on education and educators caused me to reflect on my own career as a high school and then a college teacher. I realized during my ruminations that in education I had a subject close to all of us.

And so today it is the process of education that interests me: the process of undergraduate education most of all. And it is about that process that I intend finally to draw some conclusions today. But I shall move to these conclusions somewhat circuitously and begin by telling you three personal stories, accounts of incidents that have made me think long and seriously about the nature of education in America, especially undergraduate education.

Each of these stories illustrates a widely held, but usually unacknowledged, myth about the nature of American education, a myth that, when carefully examined, falls under its own weight. Each story too points to its own moral, the adoption of which may lead us to be better educators. Thus I have titled these remarks: "Education: Myths and Morals."

The first story comes from a personal experience of several years ago in South Carolina, when I was reading over my student evaluations for a theatre history survey class. I was perplexed to see that, once again, my undergraduate students had marked me down in my knowledge of subject matter. Their grading perplexed me because, in all modesty, knowledge of field is probably my greatest strength as an undergraduate teacher. On other factors like "warm and supportive" or "readily available outside of class to be a friend," I have stunning deficiencies. And so, I asked myself, why do my students regularly mark me lowest in the area that is, in fact, my strong suit? I decided to do a little sleuthing.

I asked some of my students about their perceptions, and I think I discovered the answer to my question. One student reminded me that in class I often said things like "I don't know"; another that I often confessed that "there are several possible answers." Such admissions of personal inadequacy put me well behind the eight ball and well behind my students' high school teachers, who had known all of these answers perfectly well and who had known how to encapsulate them into a very few words that could be easily packaged and easily retrieved for a test. This discovery led me to speculate further about what we are teaching our students and, more importantly, what we are saying to them about the nature of education.

If my experience was in any way typical, I had to conclude, we have taught our students that education is supposed to be about facts, that teachers are supposed to know those facts and give them to students to learn, and that students who learn these facts become educated.

This model of education is reminiscent of an industry. The students, our raw materials, enter an educational conveyor belt in grade one. We as teachers add packaged parts at each of twelve discrete stations, after which some of these end products are distributed here and there into our society to perform fairly routine tasks until they die. Other end products, perhaps smarter or perhaps merely richer, are placed in a second, shorter, but more intense, assembly line where the process is repeated until these final products are stamped with some label of quality: a standard cut B.S., a choice cut M.A., a prime cut Ph.D. In this model of education, knowledge is assumed to be discrete bundles of data, facts; and so learning is the systematic acquisition of these bundles, and teaching is their efficient distribution. According to this view, a well-educated person is one who has lots of bundles.

This analysis of my personal experience led me to realize that, probably inadvertently, we as teachers have perpetrated a myth about education. Myth #1, simply stated, holds that *Education is a commodity, and students are consumers*.

Although widely held, this myth can be easily debunked if we simply consider our own experiences as students, teachers, and scholars. My experience, and I'm sure yours as well, suggests that one does not get an education as one gets an apple or a car; rather one pursues an education as one swims against a current toward an ever-receding shore. A person is not labelled educated because of the number of facts accumulated in a course or in a lifetime; rather people are considered educated to the degree that they can understand the interrelationships and complexities that are only dimly visible through the facts. Thus, education is not best described by models that recall factories and products but by metaphors that point to motion—to change rather than stasis, energy rather than objects, becoming rather than being. By exposing the first myth, that education is a commodity and students consumers, the first story leads to a moral: Moral #1: *Education is experienced not as a destination but as a journey; not as a finding but as a seeking.*

My second story is also based on experiences in my theatre history classes, and it is also true. Although the problem I am going to describe surfaces at several points during the survey course, I will focus on only one instance, the teaching of the origins of theatre and drama.

Over the years, I have found that if I ask almost any undergraduate student to tell me how drama or theatre came into being, I will hear some version of the following: Western theatre and drama evolved from religious rituals devoted to the worship of the god Dionysos; theatre came into being when an actor (perhaps named Thespis) stepped out from the chorus and engaged in impersonation. This particular version of truth is still being recited in most high school textbooks and in many college classrooms. Is it true?

Since at least the 1930s, there has been mounting evidence to suggest that it is not. For example, our earliest account of the origins of drama, the one set forth by Aristotle in his *Poetics*, makes no mention of Dionysos, no mention of religion, no mention of ritual, and no mention of Thespis. But perhaps Aristotle did not know much about the origins of theatre and drama; he was, after all, living some two hundred years after the supposed event in an age before printing, when information from the past was uncommon and suspect.

Let us therefore examine other kinds of evidence for corroboration, and let us use common sense. From what we know of Dionysiac worship, the ceremonies were most often marked by frenzied, irrational, and intoxicating activity. Tragedy, on the other hand, is still noted for its controlled intellectualism and rational solemnity. How could a ritual marked by revelry be reasonably supposed to transmogrify into an art work whose language, character, content, and form are noted for their quiet dignity? Moreover, if rituals dedicated to Dionysos were the source of tragedy, why do no remnants of such a ritual appear in the tragedies? Why, to cite just one example, does Dionysos occur in tragedy so seldom and so peripherally? Then there is the matter of the ritual itself. Although many religious rituals existed in Greece, few of them were dramatic, and, of those that were dramatic, none that we know of was devoted to the god Dionysos.

In my history classes I have tried to raise such doubts, to offer alternate theories, encourage comparisons among theories, and comparisons between theories and the evidence on which they are based. But usually when I have raised questions about what the students know and how they have come to know it, their reactions have been very discouraging. Most students become annoyed, some even become angry. They do not want to entertain such untidiness. Their attitude seems to be that they have their answer, and they want to hang on to it. They know a fact, and they don't want to lose it. That the fact may be false does not matter. Better to possess an inaccurate fact than to juggle ambiguities. Better to have a bundle in the luggage of education than to bump into a question mark on the swim toward truth.

This personal experience and my thinking about its implications has led me to see that many of us as teachers have promoted, again probably unconsciously, an even more serious myth about the nature of education. Myth #2: *Education is about answers, not questions.*

But again, by looking closely at the case of the origins of theatre, we can see all too clearly what is wrong with a view of education that focusses on answers. Available evidence suggests now that theatre probably did not arise from a religious ritual devoted to the god Dionysos; that is, our widely accepted fact may be wrong.

Given this situation, an apt student might reasonably be expected to ask this question: How could the popular version of the origins of theatre have gained such widespread acceptance on the basis of such flimsy evidence? In trying to answer this question, one would discover that the writings of Friedrich Nietzsche and Sir James Frazer were enormously popular at the very time that the first influential works in dramatic and theatrical history were being written, that is, in the late nineteenth and early twentieth centuries. One would discover, too, that at about the same time the ideas of Charles Darwin and the cultural anthropologists were causing extraordinary controversy and excitement. One would find further that the pervasiveness of these ideas and the writings about them had caused words like *Dionysos* and *ritual* and *religion* and *evolution* to be thick in the air at the very time that our early theatre historians were writing. A thoughtful student might even begin to suspect that the popular explanation of the origins of theatre grew not out of the evidence pursuant to the event itself but out of the assumptions that historians, writing over two thousand years after the event, brought to the question.

This observation, if correct, would then logically lead a student to pose yet another question: Given that the writings of Nietzsche, Frazer, Darwin, and the cultural anthropologists are not so pervasive today, why has the popular view of the origins persisted in spite of the conflicting evidence? The pursuit of that question would lead us into some rather depressing conclusions about professors and colleges, and so I do not wish to pursue it today.

Rather, I will note that this story and its analysis leads tidily to the second moral, a moral that debunks the myth that education is about answers; Moral #2: *Answers change, questions persist.*

My third and last story comes not from the classroom but from research that I undertook with a colleague on the history of the teaching of acting in American colleges and universities, a study recently published in *Communication Education.* As part of my research, I met a man named Ted Cloak, a person with an enviable record of achievement. For example, he taught actors who went on to work at the Guthrie in Minneapolis, at Joe Papp's in New York, at ACT in San Francisco, in repertory companies of LA, Seattle, and Milwaukee. He taught directors and producers who moved on to the Dudley Riggs Workshop and the Arizona Civic Theatre. Ted Cloak edited a volume of plays, toured Europe on a Rockefeller grant, and was among the first in this country to direct the plays of Ionesco, Brecht, and Beckett, and to teach the acting theories of Constantin Stanislavski.

Popular wisdom would have it that Professor Cloak was on the faculty of Yale or Carnegie, or that he served at a League School or perhaps a prestigious research university. In fact, however, this remarkable teacher and theatre artist was one of three members of the faculty at Lawrence University in Appleton, Wisconsin. He would now be a member of SCA's Small College Caucus of the Senior College and University Section.

This story clearly points to what may be the cruellest educational myth of all. Myth #3: *Bigger is better.*

Although widely held, especially by faculty teaching in large schools, this myth, like the others, will not hold up under scrutiny. Consolidating neighborhood schools into a single comprehensive high school did not noticeably improve the education of adolescents. Directors of graduate programs recruit theatre students from DePauw University with its three-person faculty, at least as eagerly as those from Indiana University, a few miles up the road and two dozen faculty larger. Superintendents of Texas public schools, when given a choice between a drama teacher from any one of the large state universities or from the much smaller Trinity University, will usually opt for the Trinity graduate, I'm told.

The reasons for this puzzling phenomenon are doubtless complex, but at least one deserves our immediate attention. Education, as well conceived some time ago, was a teacher at one end of a log and a student at the other. Notice, the metaphor did not put a teacher at one end of a log and three hundred students at the other, nor a student at one end and a gta [graduate teaching assistant] at the other. Nor did the image provide for a student's floating aimlessly on a log waiting for a Tuesday or Thursday when a teacher would come into view; or for a teacher to mount the end of the log only when it did not interfere with off-campus consulting. Rather the image suggests a continuous interaction between a teacher and a learner.

Here surely is part of the answer to our puzzle. In too many large research institutions, undergraduates get to watch while important teachers give lectures and gifted graduate students participate in research. Thus, although the undergraduate students are exposed to the very best minds in the field, their role as undergraduate in those institutions is often the largely passive one of observer. In small programs, on the other hand, when there are no graduate students and very few faculty members, undergraduate students necessarily assume major responsibilities both in the classroom and outside it. They necessarily take on positions of leadership and seek out specialized information. Their role is, necessarily, an active one—of seeker, of doer. Bigger is not better, then, in part because education is not passive; it is interactive. The moral of this story is clear: Learning defines teaching; that is, the student not the teacher is the proper focus of education.

What do these stories, the myths and morals, taken together teach us about the nature of higher education? They all seem to suggest that we have misplaced our emphasis. We tend to talk about information when we might better talk about inquiry; we talk of answers when we should stress questions; of teachers, when students are the real issue; of size, when quality is the point.

The stories, myths, and morals all suggest that we should do more to make students do more, that we should help them learn to ask questions, to help them seek out better evidence, to understand and control their own biases, to evaluate competing positions, and then to ask more questions—about the evidence, about themselves, their reasoning, and the answers they have inherited.

This view of education, although I believe correct, will not be a popular one, because it turns education into a personally upsetting, even threatening activity. It makes education a deeply uncomfortable activity that is forever replacing certainty with uncertainty, answers with questions, the known with the unknown, an activity that is forever about change and seldom about the status quo. And it makes education not merely personally unsettling, but also socially unsettling—even subversive—for its job so conceived is not to validate the centers of authority and power but to probe and prick such centers. Its goal is not merely to transmit the values (the answers) of a culture, but also to question those values (answers).

And here is where I would disagree with the William Bennetts. Like Bennett, I want to teach the traditions of Western culture, but I want to teach them in ways that will expand them, not enshrine them. I want to teach them in ways that will lead students to discover the contributions that women and blacks and developing nations made to our heritage and to our current prosperity. I want to teach them in ways that will lead students to grasp the very complex reasons why these contributions did not become an established part of our curricula. In sum, I want to educate students for the shrinking world of the twenty-first century, not the expanding world of the nineteenth.

INVESTING IN THE YOUNG[1]
DONALD KENNEDY[2]

At midday on July 18, 1986, President Donald Kennedy of Stanford University delivered an address in which he emphasized the importance of investing in the future of young people. The setting for the speech was unusual: an outdoor, lakeside area in a redwood grove. The site, Bohemian Grove, is located near Monte Rio, California. Kennedy's audience was also somewhat different, consisting of approximately 200 male business executives, some retired, participating in a retreat.

Kennedy probably was well-known to most of his California listeners. Not only had he served as president of prestigious Stanford University for six years, since 1980, but he had also established a reputation as a brilliant scientific researcher and gifted educator during a 17-year tenure (1960–1977) as a Stanford faculty member. In addition, he had won the respect of consumer groups and drug lobbies for his handling of controversial issues during a two-year term (1977–1979) as commissioner of the federal Food and Drug Administration. The *New York Times*, in an editorial on his departure from the FDA, called him "its best commissioner in a long time." (July 2, 1979) After returning to Stanford, he was appointed in June 1980 as the university's eighth president, to the surprise of almost no one. Since then, Kennedy has continued to be outspoken on pressing public issues relating to education, science, and research. (See *Representative American Speeches* for 1983–84, p. 63, and 1985–86, p. 156.)

In his speech at Bohemian Grove, after commenting on the inspiring setting among the redwoods, Kennedy stated that he wished to talk about images that represent ourselves and our values. Specifically, he said, he wanted to "talk today about the disparity between our images and reality."

> It is a story of two portraits. One is of the America we believe ourselves to be. It is a self-portrait that contains elements of our strongest historical traditions—it is a likeness full of robustness, vigor, and above all of youth. The other is different. It takes its form from various contemporary measures of what we are actually doing, as distinct from what we *say* we are doing. A more shadowy and indistinct likeness, it is also, I am afraid, less flattering.

Kennedy organized his speech in a problem-solution pattern. The problem, he argued, was that the country really does not care as much about the future as it thinks, as demonstrated by insufficient attention to education, to the distribution of society's resources, and to science and "our responsibility for innovation." He noted that the failure to invest adequately in the young is one for which our successors will have to pay. He then proposed remedies that he thought would solve the problem.

[1]Delivered at a retreat at an outdoor site in the Bohemian Grove, located near Monte Rio, California, to approximately 200 business executives at midday on July 18, 1986.
[2]For biographical sketch, see Appendix.

Donald Kennedy's speech: It is a pleasure and an honor to address you today. My previous incursions at Bohemia have involved the delightful foolishness of Big Game night, trading identities with my friend Chancellor Mike Heyman, and enjoying the wry tasteful witticisms of coach Joe Kapp. But this is clearly different: the post-prandial hour and the sylvan setting suggest something more uplifting. What I have for you today is not exactly that. But it will, I promise, fit within the constraints decreed by your leadership with regard to brevity; and it will be no more somber than the circumstances require. Scant reassurance, I concede.

First, just one word about the setting. How is it that we like the redwoods so much? They are big, of course, and majestic. They are old, old enough to have personal experience, if that is not too outlandish to apply to a tree, with a time at which grizzly bear, Tule elk, antelope, and cougars were all regular visitors to this grove and its surroundings. But what I like best about the redwoods is a kind of self-sufficiency they possess. In the coast range valleys one of these trees, with its tens of thousands of needles, can condense enough moisture out of a fog to create a steady drip, equal to perhaps ten inches of rainfall over the course of a year. Their self-watering supports summer streamflow, creating life where none would otherwise exist.

Majestic, vigorous, self-sufficient, it is no wonder that the coast redwoods have such symbolic appeal to Americans. We are, after all, great ones for developing such images of ourselves. But today I want to talk about the disparity between our images and reality.

It is a story of two portraits. One is of the America we believe ourselves to be. It is a self-portrait that contains elements of our strongest historical traditions—it is a likeness full of robustness, vigor, and above all of youth. The other is different. It takes its form from various contemporary measures of what we are actually doing, as distinct from what we say we are doing. A more shadowy and indistinct likeness, it is also, I am afraid, less flattering.

What are some of the main features of the first portrait, the one we like well enough to hang?

First, we think of ourselves as a nation that praises intelligence, nurtures literacy, and fosters the highest achievements of human intellect. We are justly proud of having provided an educational system that spreads its benefits in an egalitarian fashion, yet rewards excellence and pushes young people to the highest levels of accomplishment. We cite the large percentage of our citizens who graduate from high school, and the impressive proportion who eventually receive post-secondary education. We see ourselves as seriously engaged in educational experimentation and improvement, recalling, for example, the significant high-school curriculum reforms in mathematics and science of the 1960s. So in the educational cultivation of our human resources, we find much to praise, or, at least, to remember.

Second, we see ourselves as a youth-oriented society, in the best sense of that phrase. We believe we are sensitive to the needs of the young; Heaven knows we are susceptible enough to their fads! A look at contemporary advertising or at almost any indicator of popular national culture suggests our concern with youthfulness. We often say that the young represent our future, and thus persuade ourselves that we are paying them a great deal of attention.

Third, we see ourselves as a people who have mastered science and technology and employed them to gain enormous improvements in our national life; the strain of "Yankee ingenuity" runs strong in our self-image. We are proud of our inventiveness, and we think of ourselves as a nation that invests heavily in science and technology and then exports the results to less fortunate nations. Part of the notion of American know-how is that we are willing to tend the health of scientific institutions, and keep them strong for our successors; and we are proud to have chosen to do most of our basic science in the universities, so that we train tomorrow's scientists as we do today's research.

This self-portrait adds up to something, a portrait of the investing society. My colleague, the economist Victor Fuchs, would say that it displays a future time preference, it is characterized by an ability to wait for gratification instead of wanting it now.

Well, I'm afraid the makers of TV commercials and the keepers of the statistics may be wiser than the rest of us. The former offer us endless versions of having it all, now; and the latter have compiled a self-portrait a whole lot less encouraging than the one I just gave you. Let's examine this deeper likeness:

First, what is the real picture with respect to our regard for literacy and for the education of our ablest young people—the human resources on which our future will depend? Our national literacy figures have slumped badly in relation to those for other "developed" countries. Only 30% of our 17-year-olds are now classified as "adept" readers—competent enough to continue to college, or to cope in business or government work environments. Worse, only 16% of black and 20% of Hispanic 17-year-olds qualified by this standard. And in the dozen years between 1970 and 1982, average scores on the Scholastic Aptitude Test, given each year to college-bound high-school seniors, dropped by 40 points, even after correcting for the social and economic backgrounds of the test-takers. The small rebounds in the past two years may be a source of hope, but it is too early to tell.

Worse still, we have seen a flight from teaching careers on the part of our most capable young people. In the early 1980s it had gotten so bad that the average SAT scores of those students intending to go into teaching averaged nearly 100 points below those for college-bound seniors generally. That was just part of a more generalized mistrust of public service occupation, an attitude encouraged by the corrosive recent tendency of candidates for elective office, and others, to heap scorn on governmental organizations and civil servants whenever they can. Bureaucracy-bashing is a bad national habit, and it may have given us a lost generation in terms of public service. In the world of education, bureaucracy-bashing had taken the form of criticizing schools and teachers for everything that is wrong, instead of wondering whether society may be asking them to do too much for too little.

The excellent recent report by the Carnegie Forum on Education and the Economy, called *A Nation Prepared*, has given us a more thoughtful diagnosis. We are simply underinvested. We call teaching a profession, yet pay teachers and treat them as though they were blue-collar workers. There is virtually no federal leadership in innovation and curriculum reform, states and local districts are at war over control, and there is little opportunity for the best teachers to advance and to share their special knowledge in a productive way. It is hardly surprising that the dropout statistics are so disappointing, and that performance indicators—even for the best students—are lower than a decade ago.

Thus, although we give the appearance of a nation in which the development of intellectual resources is a matter of deep concern, we have deteriorated seriously in the measures by which nations are judged in that respect.

And more generally, to turn to the second feature of the portrait, our advertised orientation toward youth is belied by our national pattern of expenditures. In recent years, perhaps without really meaning to, we have redirected our society's resources away from the young, and toward those at the other end of the life cycle.

In 1970, for example, approximately equal shares of the GNP in the United States were spent on health and education. A dozen years later, expenditures on health had grown 50 percent larger than those for education. Even considering that the proportion of the elderly in the population increased during this period, the enormous shift of expenditures from the young—for the most part the objects of education—to the elderly—who receive the largest fraction of health-care dollars—represents a significant change in national policy.

Expenditures for social welfare have been shifted in the same direction. Comparisons are hard to make, but by some estimates more than 30 percent of the budget is now spent on older Americans, while just 3 to 5% is spent on children. The consequences are not surprising. For example, the proportion of Americans over 65 who live in poverty was reduced from 24% to 15% between 1970 and 1982. During that same period, though, the proportion of those under 14 who live in poverty grew from 16% to 23%. Thus the positions of elderly and young Americans with respect to this critical social indicator were exactly reversed in just a dozen years.

But what about the last feature, the vigor of our scientific venture. Surely that is realistic!

Well, by some measures it is. Through the first part of this century, we took remarkably good care of American science. Some of the early history is inspiring. It begins in the 1920s with a man who enjoyed this grove, and in whose house I am now privileged to live. Herbert Hoover argued, as Secretary of Commerce is the mid-1920s, that U.S. industry needed the ideas as well as the trained scientists it could obtain from universities. He said this, among other things:

A nation with an output of $50 billion annually in commodities which could not be produced but for the discoveries of pure science, could well afford, it would seem, to put back a hundredth of 1% as an assurance of further progress.

Hoover's rhetoric did not convince the industrial America of 1925. But his ideas did result in more federal funding for basic science in the universities during the 1930s, and may well have helped prepare us for the remarkable events that followed World

War II. In the short period of time from 1946 to 1951, we transformed an extraordinary apparatus of military research into a peacetime enterprise located largely in the universities, and funded primarily by government sources, initially the Department of Defense, then the National Institutes of Health, and ultimately a new agency created just for the support of basic research, the National Science Foundation.

This system has worked admirably; over the next three decades, it brought us a steady stream of innovation, new technologies, and productivity improvements. And it has lifted American science to the very top. Two and a half years ago the King of Sweden gave Nobel Prizes to five persons in the four research disciplines, and all were American. Those of you who admit to some California chauvinism will be pleased to know that three were Californians. It was the second time in seven years that Americans had swept the research prizes, a feat previously accomplished only by Germany in 1905. After the first U.S. sweep, the noted Swedish biologist Sune Bergstrom explored the U.S. success and concluded that it was due to what he called "the democracy of American science," the unique decision to locate graduate training and research in the same places, so that the experience and wisdom of senior scientists could blend with the enthusiasm and vigor of their apprentices. No other industrial democracy has made that commitment, signalled by the location of two-thirds of our basic research in the universities; and none has succeeded as we have.

But we are now harvesting the fruits of a crop planted and grown two decades earlier. Good science requires patient husbandry, and matures slowly. Today's rewards properly belong to the caretakers of the past, whereas we, you and I, are responsible for the future. Thus our continuing Nobel harvest is a little illusory, like a late Indian summer crop that one can't be sure of next year. As to our investment in science, support has been dropping rapidly; and in 1983, the last year for which complete data are available, we spent only 1.9% of our GNP on nonmilitary research and development. By comparison, Japan invested 2.6%, West Germany 2.5%. Although program commitments for basic research have held up fairly well, the capital base for doing that work—the facilities and equipment—have suffered serious erosion.

That phenomenon can be traced back nearly 20 years. Through most of the 1960s, federal support of basic science was adequate to handle both the operating side and the modest capital demands associated with most scientific work. Toward the end of the 1960s, two things happened. First, we witnessed the end of federal support for the construction of research facilities. Second, because of rapid technological changes in the doing of science, the demand for new and more sophisticated equipment rose dramatically. Yet for FY 1984, the last for which complete data were available, the total federal investment in R&D plant in universities is projected at just $50 million.

Herbert Hoover would have approved of the way the private sector is trying to fill in. At Stanford, we are trying to work away at a staggering shortfall of research facilities, at least a third of a billion dollars' worth, mostly concentrated in the science and engineering areas to the west of the main Quadrangle, and in the Medical School. Industry and private individuals have been responsible for nearly a hundred million dollars' worth of recovery so far. And especially farsighted foundations are occasionally recognizing that capital needs demand special attention right now. The landmark gift of the W. M. Keck Foundation of Los Angeles to build the new CalTech/UC telescope is an especially encouraging case in point. Still, the size of the task is simply too large to be undertaken without public sector leadership.

And to the limited extent that this problem is now being addressed by government, it is being addressed in the wrong way, and that gives rise to a new problem all its own. The budget measure that passed the Congress a few weeks ago added $56 million in facilities as part of the defense appropriation. But those facilities were not ones that had survived competitive scientific scrutiny within the agency. Instead, they were add-ons, earmarked for institutions in particular states by their friendly representatives without examination for scientific merit. The projects could be good, but we can't know. If Congress continues to make direct appropriations of this kind based on political influences rather than merit review, American science will be in deep trouble. It needs help; but the wrong kind will sap public confidence and invite mediocrity.

Thus in all three aspects of investing in the young—education, how we distribute society's resources, and how we treat science and our responsibility for innovation—our self-portrait is not really as we see it. And it is not the picture of a nation that cares as much about the future as it thinks. For the social cost of failure to invest adequately in the young is not one we pay today; our successors will pay it; in doing so they will have to cheat their own successors; and so on.

Thus we find ourselves entering a trap. If political neglect of the young and their training continues, we will only enhance intergenerational dependence. The youngsters we slight today will become more dependent, less productive adults later on, and so they will require even more of the societal resources that should go to their children. Only ingenuity and productivity improvement can get us out of that trap; but those things depend on the strength of our educational and scientific systems, which are part of our misinvestment pattern. Scientific and technological decay, political neglect of education and the schools, the juvenilization of poverty are related; all form a trend in America's political economy that could, if we do not arrest it, become a death spiral.

What can we do about it? I have a few remedies to propose.

At the center of the problem is the inability of this government to formulate and pursue a strategy of investment. It is not obvious why that is so difficult; nonetheless, investment is a word that is simply never used or thought about in connection with congressional budgeting and finance. It must become a shaping force, and I believe that must start with the tax system.

We must develop better tax treatment for encouraging investment, especially in research and other ventures that yield future benefits. Equally, we need to explore new ways to tax personal consumption and to spare personal investment. Neither the present tax structure, nor the one emerging from the spasm of reform we have been witnessing, provides adequate incentives to put investment first.

And we should examine our patterns of national expenditure more carefully, with an eye to payoff not tomorrow or next week but in the more distant future. The most highly leveraged expenditures we can make are those on the young, who can repay the investment over long lifetimes of enhanced personal contributions. Nowhere is that more critical than for our very brightest young people, those who carry the creative intellectual spark that could produce dramatic changes in our knowledge of ourselves or our universe.

Perhaps we need a new kind of instrument for evaluating how each national policy affects the welfare of different age segments of the population. Call it a demographic impact statement. If we had one, it would surely raise some interesting questions about current policy. For example, why is all aid to college students means-tested, whereas Medicare and Social Security payments to the elderly are entitlements given without regard to financial need? And why are social security payments indexed to inflation, whereas fellowships and traineeships for young scientists are not?

Surely, too, the government would find it easier to make wise investment decisions if we could do something to improve the way in which Congress budgets expenditures. In our present system, recurring obligations (like the salary associated with a position) and one-time expenditures (like new buildings) are treated just the same. As a result, the Congress can reach a reduction target by taking out one major capital item just as easily as by eliminating dozens of positions. Which will they choose? The big ticket, naturally. It is a formula well calculated to disadvantage capital investment. A separation between recurring or "base" expenditures and capital outlays in the Federal budget process would help to provide a national discipline for taking care of our infrastructure.

Finally, the very richest opportunities for improvement lie in the area of science and education, on which we depend for the human and instrumental resources to supply an innovative society.

Our past neglect in this area can be made up for, if we act quickly. But who will do it? As I have said, industry is helping, but the task is too large and their need to satisfy other, short-term demands from their own investors is too great. The universities have fairly impressive endowments, and you are likely all too aware of their eagerness to grow them! But although to some that makes the universities look rich, they are feeling poor. They have grown their endowments only a little faster than inflation, and it is a surprising fact that the endowments of Harvard and Stanford both contribute a lower proportion of the operating budgets of those institutions than they did fifteen years ago.

Well, who can do it? The White House Science Council and its chairman, Dave Packard, have supplied an answer as well as a diagnosis. The council said in its recently issued report: "science and technology are critical to our future. Nations everywhere are investing in these capabilities. We conclude that we must rethink and, in many ways rebuild the critically important interactions between universities, government, and industry that have served this nation so well in the past. The federal government/university relationship is too fundamental to the maintenance of our national science and technology base to be taken for granted, and the industry/university partnership is emerging as critical to exploring that base in order to compete in the world marketplace. One conclusion is clear: our universities today simply cannot respond to society's expectations for them or discharge their national responsibilities in research and education without substantially increased support."

Only the federal government can manage the sort of financial intervention the Packard panel is advocating.

And its words take us back to where Hoover began, with the educational institutions of America, particularly its research universities. Their capacity to support scientific work must be shored up by direct government support for building and equipment, and by the payment of full audited indirect as well as direct costs of doing sponsored research. We will suffer a dreadful setback if the awarding of funds for research facilities comes to be regarded by the Congress as a new opportunity—like the rivers and harbors appropriation—for spreading wealth to their own districts and their own friends. The principle that scientific merit and not geography or some other factor should govern such events is the best guarantee of quality in our scientific enterprise.

What I have just been talking about, you may say, is only a piece of the American future, just a piece of one dimension of domestic policy, just one of a number of areas important to our national security. That is true. But I hope you will ask yourselves this question. If it is not to be our young scientists and their future work that will gain us a secure place among the nations and a better life for our citizens, then what will it be instead? And, more generally, how can we fail to invest adequately in the successor generation given what the stakes are? I cannot believe we will allow this to happen. For the result—the entirely unacceptable result—would be that forty years or so from now a generation will stand where we are now, knowing that things are, for the very first time in American history, worse than they were for their fathers.

APPENDIX

Biographical Notes

BENNETT, WILLIAM JOHN (1943–). Born, Brooklyn, New York; B.A., Williams College, 1965; Ph.D., University of Texas, 1970; J.D., Harvard University, 1971; Litt. D., Gonzaga University, 1982; H.H.D., Franklin College, 1982; L.H.D., University of New Hampshire, 1982; LL.D., Williams College, 1983; assistant to president, Boston University, 1972–76; executive director, National Humanities Center, 1976–79; associate professor, North Carolina State University, Raleigh, 1979–81; chairman, National Endowment for the Humanities, 1981–85; secretary, United States Department of Education, 1985– . (See also *Current Biography*, September, 1985.)

BOK, DEREK (1930–). Born, Bryn Mawr, Pennsylvania; B.A., Stanford University, 1951; J.D., Harvard University, 1954; M.A., George Washington University, 1958; Fulbright Scholar, Paris, 1954–55; served to 1st lieutenant AUS, 1956–58; faculty, Harvard University Law School, 1958– ; professor, Harvard Law School, 1961– ; dean, Harvard Law School, 1968–71; president, Harvard University, 1971– ; member, American Council on Education, Institute of Medicine, American Philosophical Society, Phi Beta Kappa, Phi Kappa Sigma; trustee, Committee for Economic Development; fellow, American Academy of Arts and Sciences; editor, with Archibald Coy, *Cases and Materials on Labor Law*, 1962; author, *Labor and the American Community* (with John T. Dunlop), 1970; *Beyond the Ivory Tower: Social Responsibilities of the Modern University*, 1982; contributor, *In the Public Interest*, 1980. (See also *Current Biography*, July, 1971.)

CHURCH, FRANK FORRESTER IV (1948–). Born, Boise, Idaho; B.A., with distinction, Stanford University, 1970; M. Div., *magna cum laude*, Harvard University, 1974, Ph.D., 1978; minister, Unitarian Church of All Souls, New York City, 1978– ; author, more than twenty books, including *Father and Son: A Personal Biography of Senator Frank Church of Idaho by His Son*, 1985, *The Devil and Dr. Church*, 1986, *Entertaining Angels*, 1987, *The Essential Tillich*, 1987; articles on New Testament studies, the history of early Christianity, the history of liberal religion, and contemporary theological and ethical topics.

GILLESPIE, PATTI PEETE (1938–). Born, Bowling Green, Kentucky; B.A., University of Kentucky, 1958; M.A., Western Kentucky University, 1964; Ph.D., Indiana University, 1970; assistant professor of speech and dramatic art, University of Iowa, 1970–74; associate professor and head of department of theatre and speech, University of South Carolina, 1974–82; professor and chairman of department of communication arts and theatre, University of Maryland, 1982– ; visiting professor, Bowling

160

Green State University, 1980-81; Mitchell distinguished visiting professor, Trinity University, San Antonio, spring 1987; president, Association of Communication Administration, 1979; president, Speech Communication Association, 1987; member and officer of American Theatre Association and Southern Speech Communication Association; author, *Speech: An Important Skill* (with Robert Kemp), 1975, *The Enjoyment of Theatre* (with Kenneth Cameron), 1980, *Western Theatre* (with Kenneth Cameron), 1984, and many articles in communication, theatre, and college administration journals and publications.

HARRIMAN, PAMELA DIGBY (1920-). Born, Farnborough, England; came to United States, 1959; naturalized, 1971; Bachelor of Domestic Science-Economy, Downham College, England, 1937; post-graduate work, Sorbonne, Paris, 1937-38; with ministry of supply, London, 1942-43; with Churchill Club for American Servicemen, 1943-46; journalist, Beaverbrook Press, Europe, 1946-49; member, national finance council, Democratic National Committee; member, Democratic House and Senate Council; co-chair, Democratic Congressional Dinner, 1979; founder, Democrats for the 80's; trustee, Rockefeller University, National Gallery of Art; advisory committee, World Rehabilitation Foundation; board of directors, Mary W. Harriman Foundation; member of various philanthropic foundations; Democratic Woman of the Year, Woman's National Democratic Club, 1980.

JACOB, JOHN E. (1934-). Born, Trout, Louisiana; B.A., Howard University, 1957, M.S.W., 1963; caseworker, then child welfare casework supervisor, Baltimore Department of Public Welfare, 1960-65; began work with National Urban League in 1965 as Director of Education and Youth Incentives at the Washington Urban League, where he later filled a series of administrative positions, Acting Executive Director, 1968-70; Director of Community Organization Training, Eastern Regional Office, National Urban League, 1970; Executive Director, San Diego Urban League, 1970-75; President, Washington Urban League, 1975-79; Executive Director, National Urban League, 1979-81, President, 1982- ; vice chairman, trustees, Howard University, 1971- ; member, National Association of Social Workers, Academy of Certified Social Workers; awards, Achievement Award, Eastern Province, Kappa Alpha Psi, 1976, Whitney M. Young Memorial Award, Washington Urban League, 1979, Public Service Award, United Black Fund, Washington Urban League, 1979, Outstanding Community Service Award, Howard University School of Social Work Alumni Association, 1979. (See also *Current Biography*, February, 1986.)

KENNEDY, DONALD (1931-). Born, New York City; B.A., Harvard University, 1952, M.A., Ph.D., 1956; faculty member, Syracuse University, 1956-60; faculty member, Stanford University, 1960-77, professor of biological sciences, 1965-77, chairman of the department, 1965-72; senior consultant, Office of Scientific and Technological Policy, Executive Office of the President, 1976; commissioner, Federal Drug Administration, 1977-79; vice president and provost, Stanford University, 1979-80, president, 1980- ; board of overseers, Harvard University, 1970-76; fellow, American Academy of Arts and Sciences; member, National

Academy of Sciences, American Physiology Society, Society of General Physiologists, American Society of Zoologists, Society of Experimental Biology (U.K.); author (with W. H. Telfer), *The Biology of Organisms*, 1965; editor, *The Living Cell*, 1966, *From Cell to Organism*, 1967; editorial board, *Journal of Experimental Zoology*, 1965-71, *Journal of Comparative Physiology*, 1965-76, *Journal of Neurophysiology*, 1969-75, *Science*, 1973-77. (See also *Current Biography*, July, 1984.)

KENNEDY, EDWARD MOORE (1932-   ). Born, Boston, Massachusetts; A.B., Harvard University, 1956; student, International Law School, The Hague, The Netherlands, 1958; LL.B., University of Virginia, 1959; honorary degrees, thirteen institutions; admitted, Massachusetts bar, 1959; assistant district attorney, Suffolk County, Massachusetts, 1961-62; U.S. senator, Masssachusetts, 1962-   ; former assistant majority leader, U.S. Senate; chairman, judiciary committee, 1979-81; member, labor and human resources committee, 1981-   ; president, Joseph P. Kennedy Jr. Foundation, 1961-   ; member, board of trustees, universities, hospitals, libraries, the Boston Symphony, John F. Kennedy Center for the Performing Arts, and Robert F. Kennedy Memorial Foundation; named one of ten outstanding young men in United States by Junior Chamber of Commerce, 1967; author, *Decisions for a Decade*, 1968, *In Critical Condition: The Crisis in America's Health Care*, 1972, *Our Day and Generation*, 1979, *Freeze: How You Can Help Prevent Nuclear War* (with Mark O. Hatfield), 1979. (See also *Current Biography*, October, 1978.)

KOOP, CHARLES EVERETT (1916-   ). Born, Brooklyn, New York; B.A., Dartmouth College, 1937; M.D., Cornell University, 1941; Sc.D., University of Pennsylvania, 1947; LL.D., Eastern Baptist College, 1960; M.D. (honorary), University of Liverpool, 1968; L.H.D., Wheaton College, 1973; D.Sc., Gwynedd Mercy College, 1978; intern, Pennsylvania Hospital, 1941-42; surgeon in chief, Children's Hospital of Philadelphia, 1948-   ; with University of Pennsylvania School of Medicine, 1942-   , professor, 1959-   ; fellow in surgery, Boston Children's Hospital, 1946; consultant, U.S. Navy, 1964-   ; director, international health, 1982-   ; Surgeon General of the U.S., 1981-   ; member, board of directors, Medical Assistance Programs, Inc., Daystar Communications, Inc., Eastern Baptist Seminary and College; fellow, American Academy of Pediatrics; decorated, chevalier Legion of Honor, France; recipient, medal, City of Marseille; Kopernicus Medal, Polish Surgical Society; William E. Ladd Gold Medal, American Academy of Pediatrics; Dennis Browne Gold Medal, British Association of Pediatric Surgeons; fellow, American College of Surgeons; president, Association of Military Surgeons of U.S., 1982; member, American Surgeons Association, Society of University Surgeons, British Association of Pediatric Surgeons, International Society of Surgery, Société Française de Chirurgie Infantile, American Medical Association, Deutschen Gesselschaft für Kinderchirurgi, Société Suisse de Chirurgie Infantile, Order Duarte, Sanchez y Mella, Dominican Republic; editor-in-chief, *Journal of Pediatric Surgery*, 1965-77; contributor to surgical, physiological, biomedical, ethical, and pediatric journals. (See also *Current Biography*, September, 1983.)

MOORE, PAUL JR. (1919-   ). Born, Morristown, New Jersey; B.A., Yale University, 1941; S.T.B., General Theological Seminary (New York City), 1949; honorary degrees, 1960, 1964; USMCR, 1941-45; recipient, Navy Cross, Silver Star, Purple Heart; member of team ministry, Grace Church, Jersey City, 1949-57; dean, Christ Church Cathedral, Indianapolis, 1957-64; suffragan bishop, Washington, D.C., 1964-70; bishop coadjuter, diocese of New York, 1970-72; bishop, 1972-   ; chairman, Delta Ministry Commission, National Council of Churches, 1964-67; Committee of Denominational Executives; member, Legal Defense Fund, NAACP, 1956-   ; urban division, National Council of the Episcopal Church, 1952-68; Foundation for Free Expression; Governor's Commission on AIDS; Inter-religious Bail Foundation; trustee, General Theological Seminary, Trinity School, Berkeley Divinity School at Yale University; fellow, Yale Corporation, 1964-   ; author, *The Church Reclaims the City*, 1970 (2d ed.), *Take a Bishop Like Me*, 1979; contributed chapters to *Viewpoints, Some Aspects of Anglican Thinking*, 1959 and *On the Battle Lines*, 1964. (See also *Current Biography*, January, 1967.)

REAGAN, RONALD WILSON (1911-   ). Born, Tampico, Illinois; B.A., Eureka College (Illinois), 1932; sports announcer, radio station WHO, Des Moines, Iowa, 1932-37; motion picture and television actor, 1937-66; program supervisor, General Electric Theater; president, Screen Actors Guild, 1947-52, 1959; captain, U.S. Air Force, 1942-45; governor, California, 1967-74; unsuccessful candidate for Republican presidential nomination, 1976; U.S. President, 1980-   ; author, *Where's the Rest of Me*, 1965 (reprint 1981 as *My Early Life*), *Abortion and the Conscience of the Nation*, 1984. (See also *Current Biography*, February, 1967 and November, 1982.)

REHNQUIST, WILLIAM HUBBS (1924-   ). Born, Milwaukee, Wisconsin; B.A., M.A., Stanford University, 1948, LL.B., 1952; M.A., Harvard University, 1949; admitted to Arizona bar; law clerk to Supreme Court Justice Robert H. Jackson, 1952-53; with Phoenix law firms of Evans, Kitchel, and Jenckes, 1953-55, Ragan and Rehnquist, 1956-57, Cunningham, Carson, and Messenger, 1957-60, and Powers and Rehnquist, 1960-69; assistant attorney-general, office of legal counsel, Department of Justice, Washington, 1969-71; associate justice, United States Supreme Court, 1971-86, Chief Justice, 1986-   ; member, National Conference of Commissioners for Uniform State Laws, 1963-69; member of United States Army Air Force, 1943-46; member of Federation of American County Bar Associations, Arizona State Bar Association, National Conference of Lawyers and Realtors, Phi Beta Kappa. Contributor to law journals and national magazines. (See also *Current Biography*, April, 1972.)

SILBER, JOHN (1926-   ). Born, San Antonio, Texas; B.A., *summa cum laude*, Trinity University, 1947; postgraduate work, Yale Divinity School, 1947-48; University of Texas Law School, 1948; M.A., Yale University, 1952, Ph.D., 1956; L.H.D., 1970, Kalamazoo College; instructor, philosophy, Yale University, 1952-55; assistant professor, philosophy, University of Texas at Austin, 1955-59, associate professor, 1959-62, professor, 1962-70, chairman of department, 1962-67, professor of arts and letters, 1967-70; president of the university and professor of philosophy and law,

Boston University, 1971-   ; visiting professor, University of Bonn, 1960; trustee, College of St. Scholastica, WGBH Educational Foundation; board of directors, Greater Boston Council of Boy Scouts of America, 1981-   ; fellow, Kings College, University of London, 1963–64; awards, Harbison award for teaching, Danforth Foundation, 1966, Fulbright research fellowship, Germany, 1959-60, Guggenheim fellowship, 1963–64; director, National Association of Independent Colleges and Universities, 1976–81; president, Southwestern Philosophical Society, 1966–67; chairman, Texas Society to Abolish Capital Punishment, 1960–69; Big Thicket national advertising committee; member, National Commission, United Methodist Higher Education, 1974–77; National Bipartisan Commission of Central America; American Philosophical Association; American Society of Political and Legal Philosophy; Aristotelian Society, Royal Institute of Philosophy; American Association of Higher Education; Phi Beta Kappa. Wilber Lucius Cross medal, Yale Graduate School, 1971; contributor to professional journals; author, *The Ethical Significance of Kant's Religion*, 1960; editor, *Religion Within the Limits of Reason Alone*, 1960, *Works in Continental Philosophy*, 1967. (See also *Current Biography*, February, 1984.)

SIMON, PAUL (1928-   ). Born, Eugene, Oregon; student, University of Oregon, 1945–46; student, Dana College, Blair, Nebraska, 1946–48; LL.D., Dana College, 1965; D. Litt., McKendree College, 1965; D.C.L., Greenville College, 1968; LL.D., Concordia College, 1968, Lincoln College, 1969, Loyola University, 1969, Valparaiso University, 1976; publisher, *Troy* (Illinois) *Tribune*, 1948–66; member, Illinois House of Representatives, 1955–63, Illinois Senate, 1963–69; lieutenant governor of Illinois, 1969–73; professor of public affairs, Sangamon State University, Springfield, 1973; member, 94th–98th Congresses from 24th District of Illinois; United States Senator from Illinois, 1985-   ; board of directors, Dana College, McKendree College; member, Lutheran Human Relations Association, NAACP, Urban League; fellow, John F. Kennedy Institute of Politics, Harvard, 1973; recipient, American Political Science Association Award, 1957; named Best Legislator 7 times; author, *Lovejoy: Martyr to Freedom*, 1964, *Lincoln's Preparation for Greatness*, 1966, *A Hungry World*, 1966, *Protestant-Catholic Marriages Can Succeed* (with Jeanne Hurley Simon), 1967, *You Want to Change the World? So Change It*, 1971, *The Glass House, The Politics of Hunger* (with Jeanne Hurley Simon), 1973, *Politics and Morality in the Nation's Capitol*, 1984; contributor, articles to periodicals. (See also *Current Biography*, March, 1975.)

TRUDEAU, GARRY B. (1948-   ). Born, New York, New York; graduate, Yale University, 1970; Yale University School of Art and Architecture; creator, *Doonesbury* comic strip; recipient, Pulitzer Prize, 1975; author, of numerous books including *For Your Fans, Rollie; The Doonesbury Chronicles; Guilty, Guilty, Guilty!; We Who Are about to Fry, Salute You: Selected Cartoons from in Search of Reagan's Brain, Vol. 2; Is This Your First Purge, Miss? Vol. 2; It's Supposed to Be Yellow, Pinhead: Selected Cartoons from You Ask for May, Settle for June, Vol. 1; The Wreck of the Rusty Nail*; playwright, *Doonesbury* (with Elizabeth Swados), 1983, *Rapmaster Ronnie, A Partisan Review*, 1984. (See also *Current Biography*, August, 1975.)

WHARTON, CLIFTON REGINALD, JR. (1926–). Born, Boston, Massachusetts; B.A., Harvard University, 1947; M.A., Johns Hopkins University, 1948; M.A., University of Chicago, 1956; Ph.D. in Economics, 1958; hon. dgs., eighteen institutions; executive trainee, American International Association of Economic and Social Development, 1948–49, program analyst, 1949–51, head, reports and analysis, 1951–53; research assistant, economics, University of Chicago, 1953–56, research associate, 1956–57; executive associate, Agriculture Development Council, 1957–58, associate, 1958–64, director American universities research program, 1964–67, vice president, 1967–69; president, Michigan State University, 1970–78; chancellor, State University of New York System, 1978–87; chairman and chief executive officer, Teachers Insurance and Annuity Association—College Retirement Equities Fund, 1987– ; visiting professor, University of Malaya, Singapore, 1958–64, Stanford University, 1964–65; member, Presidential Task Force on Agriculture in Vietnam, 1966; advisor, East Asia and Pacific State Department, 1966–69; member, Presidential mission to Latin America, 1969, Presidential Commission on World Hunger, 1978–80, National Council on Foreign Languages and International Studies, 1980–81; chairman, international food and agricultural development, State Department, 1976–83; co-chairman, Commission on Security and Economic Assistance, Department of State, 1983; board of directors, Ford Motor Company, 1973– , Time Incorporated, 1982– , Federal Reserve Bank of New York, deputy chairman, 1982– , Federated Department Stores, 1985– ; trustee, Rockefeller Foundation, 1970– , chairman, 1982– ; trustee, Overseas Development Council, 1969– , Carnegie Foundation, 1970–79, Aspen Institute of Humanistic Studies, 1980– , Committee on Economic Development, 1980– , Council on Foreign Relations, 1983– , Foreign Policy Association, 1983– , MIT Corporation, 1984– , Academy of Educational Development, 1985– ; co-author, *Patterns for Lifelong Learning*, 1973; editor, *Subsistence Agriculture and Economic Development*, 1969; contributor of articles to professional journals; member, American Economics Association, Association of Asian Studies, National Academy of Education.

WIESEL, ELIE(ZER) (1928–). Born, Sighet, Transylvania; came to U.S., 1956, naturalized; attended Sorbonne, University of Paris, 1947–50; honorary degrees, twenty-nine institutions; foreign correspondent at various times for *Yedioth Ahronoth*, Tel Aviv, Israel, *L'Arche*, Paris, France, and *Jewish Daily Forward*, New York City, 1949– ; Distinguished Professor, City College of the University of New York, New York City, 1972–76; Andrew Mellon Professor in the Humanities, Boston University, Boston, Massachusetts, 1976– ; Henry Luce Visiting Scholar, Yale University, New Haven, Connecticut; chairman, U.S. President's Commission on the Holocaust, U.S. Holocaust Memorial Council; board of directors, National Committee on American Foreign Policy, Hebrew Arts School, HUMANITAS, International Rescue Committee; board of governors, Oxford Center for Postgraduate Hebrew Studies, Ben-Gurion University of the Negev, Haifa University, Tel-Aviv University, Bar-Ilan University; board of trustees, Yeshiva University; colleague, Cathedral of St. John the Divine; member, Phi Beta Kappa; honorary chairman, National Jewish Resource Center; recipient, Prix Rivarol, 1964, Jewish Heritage Award,

Haifa University, 1965, Remembrance Award, 1965, Prix Medicis, 1968, Prix Bordin French Academy, 1972, Eleanor Roosevelt Memorial Award, New York United Jewish Appeal, 1972, American Liberties Medallion, American Jewish Committee, 1972, Martin Luther King Jr. Medallion, City College of the University of New York, 1973, Faculty Distinguished Scholar Award, Hofstra University, 1973–74, Jewish Heritage Award, B'nai B'rith, Avoda Award, Jewish Teachers Association, Humanitarian Award, B'rith Sholom, Jabotinsky Medal, State of Israel, International Literature Prize for Peace, Royal Academy, Belgium, 1983, Congressional Gold Medal, 1984, Remembrance Award, Israel Bonds, 1985, Anne Frank Award, 1985; fellow, Jewish Academy of Arts and Sciences, Timothy Dwight College, Yale University; author of twenty-three books including *Night*, 1960, *Dawn*, 1961, *The Accident*, 1962, *A Beggar in Jerusalem*, 1970, *Souls on Fire*, 1972, *The Fifth Son*, 1985. (See also *Current Biography*, February, 1986.)

CUMULATIVE SPEAKER INDEX

1980-1987

A cumulative author index to the volumes of *Representative American Speeches* for the years 1937-1938 through 1959-1960 appears in the 1959-1960 volume, for the years 1960-1961 through 1969-1970 in the 1969-1970 volume, and for 1970-1971 through 1979-1980, in the 1979-1980 volume.

Coates, J. F. 1981–82, 200–14, The future of computer data security

Cox, Archibald. 1982–83, 62–71, The best of times? The worst of times?

Csorba, Laszlo III. 1985–86, 91–101, Academic freedom or academic license?

Cuomo, M. M. 1984–85, 22–32, A case for the Democrats 1984: a tale of two cities; 1985–86, 108–20, Abraham Lincoln and our "unfinished business"

Daniel, M. T. 1984–85, 151–4, The remarkable man from Missouri: Harry S. Truman

Dyer, C. S. 1983–84, 140–152, The costs of freedom of the press

Edwards, Harry. 1983–84, 124–132, Black student-athletes: taking responsibility

Ervin, S. J. Jr. 1980–81, 61–75, Judicial verbicide: an affront to the Constitution

Ewald, W. B. Jr. 1982–83, 174–9, Man of steel, velvet, and peace: Dwight D. Eisenhower

Feinstein, Dianne. 1983–84, 99–103, Women in politics: time for a change

Ferraro, G. A. 1982–83, 198–207, Women in leadership can make a difference

Gerbner, George. 1985–86, 142–48, Children's television: a national disgrace

Gerlach, L. R. 1983–84, 104–113, Sport as part of our society

Gillespie, P. P. 1986–87, 142–9, Education: myths and morals

Glenn, J. H. Jr. 1981–82, 183–94, A time for decision

Goldenson, L. H. 1984–85, 8–15, Democracy's most important right: to vote

Gunderson, R. G. 1981–82, 172–83, Digging up Parson Weems

Haiman, F. S. 1984–85, 42–58, How fares the First Amendment?

Harriman, Pamela. 1986–87, 22–31, "The sinews of peace": remarks commemorating the 40th anniversary of Winston Churchill's 'Iron Curtain' speech

Harris, P. R. 1980–81, 35–48, Political pluralism and religious absolutism

Hart, Gary. 1982–83, 55–62, A time for economic reform

Holland, J. R. 1984–85, 79–95, A "notion" at risk: the greater crisis in American education

Hook, Sidney. 1984–85, 107–121, The humanities and the defense of a free society

Hooks, B. L. 1983–84, 81–91, Struggle on

Ilchman, A. S. 1981–82, 102–11, The public purposes of private colleges

Jacob, J. E. 1981–82, 145–50, The state of black America; 1986–87, 86–93, Two challenges: South Africa and urban education

Murphy, J. S. 1985-86, 101-107, Accuracy in Academia

Newsom, D. D. 1981-82, 33-43, What Americans want in foreign policy

Nisbet, R. A. 1985-86, 120-25, The most unbelievable thing

O'Neill, M. J. 1982-83, 97-111, The power of the press: a problem for the republic: a challenge for editors

Pepper, C. D. 1981-82, 168-71, In memory of Franklin D. Roosevelt

Quainton, A. C. E. 1980-81, 83-94, Terrorism and low-level conflict: a challenge for the 1980s

Randolph, Jennings. 1981-82, 165-8, In memory of Franklin D. Roosevelt

Reagan, R. W. 1980-81, 9-18, Inaugural address, 76-81, Welcome home!; 1981-82, 9-25, A new federalism: state of the union address; 1982-83, 8-24, Staying the course: state of the union address; 1984-85, 33-41, Second inaugural address; 1985-86, 9-19, Speech on the 40th anniversary of the United Nations; 1986-87, 8-12, Remarks at the lighting of the Statue of Liberty

Rehnquist, W. H. 1984-85, 58-71, Presidential appointments to the Supreme Court; 1986-87, 13-21, The many faces of the Bicentennial

Reston, J. B. 1983-84, 113-23, Sports and politics

Reynolds, W. A. 1983-84, 15-26, What is right with our public schools

Ritter, Bruce. 1983-84, 175-87, Broken families and homeless children

Robb, C. S. 1984-85, 205-12, Rekindling the commitment to civic responsibility

Rockefeller, David. 1985-86, 175-85, Giving: big bucks, bare basics, and blue skies

Rosenthal, A. M. 1981-82, 124-35, Acceptance of the Elijah Parish Lovejoy award

Rostow, W. W. 1982-83, 152-60, Foreign policy: the President, Congress, and public opinion

Sagan, C. E. 1983-84, 75-81, 1984 and 2001: A New Year's resolution

Saldich, A. R. 1980-81, 110-29, Electronic democracy: how television governs

Sanford, Terry. 1983-84, 45-52, Is America a leader?

Sawhill, J. C. 1980-81, 167-85, Higher education in the '80s: beyond retrenchment

Saxon, D. S. 1982-83, 112-23, The place of science and technology in the liberal arts curriculum

Scanlon, T. J. 1983-84, 153-57, Tribute to John F. Kennedy

Schlesinger, A. M. Jr. 1981-82, 161-5, In memory of Franklin D. Roosevelt; 1984-85, 154-72, Eleanor Roosevelt

Senese, D. J. 1981-82, 89-102, Can we have excellence in education?